SEX IN THE

MOVIES

By Sam Frank

A Citadel Press Book

Published by Carol Publishing Group

Library of Congress Cataloging-in-Publication Data

Frank, Sam.
  Sex in the movies.

  1. Sex in moving-pictures.   I. Title.
PN1995.9.S45F73   1986   791.43'09'09353   86-17630
ISBN 0-8065-0999-6

First Carol Publishing Group Edition 1990

A Citadel Press Book
Published by Carol Publishing Group

Editorial Offices
600 Madison Avenue
New York, NY 10022

Sales & Distribution Offices
120 Enterprise Avenue
Secaucus, NJ 07094

In Canada: Musson Book Company
A division of General Publishing Co. Limited
Don Mills, Ontario

Queries regarding rights and permissions
should be addressed to: Carol Publishing Group,
600 Madison Avenue, New York, NY 10022

Manufactured in the United States of America

10 9 8 7 6 5 4 3 2

Carol Publishing Group books are available at special
discounts for bulk purchases, for sales promotions,
premiums, fund raising, or educational use. Special
editions can also be created to specifications.
For details contact: Special Sales Department,
Carol Publishing Group, 120 Enterprise Avenue,
Secaucus, NJ 07094

DESIGNED BY LESTER GLASSNER

For J. David Kiser
Friend, confidant, collaborator.
He knows my guilty pleasures and understands them.

And for Veronica Hart
One of the most gifted actresses in America.
Veronica, honey, I hope this book persuades some mainstream
Hollywood producers to give you the big legit break you
deserve.

CONTENTS

ACKNOWLEDGMENTS

I used to think that putting together a book like this was a relatively simple process of viewing a few score movies to fill in some gaps and rounding up a few hundred choice stills at memorabilia shops. A few months of medium-hard work and presto, a commercial coffeetable book. In other cases, this might have been absolutely true, but in the case of this assignment, I couldn't have been more wrong.

In point of fact, compiling this sequel to Parker Tyler's book involved three phases, the first of which was heavy duty: sitting or skimming through over 200 movies, mainly on home video, that I either hadn't seen—some were released as I was researching this book—or which I needed to see again to refresh my memory. Thank heaven for the video industry, which has made film research a lot easier by making thousands of movies, contemporary and vintage, easily accessible and less cumbersome than expensive-to-rent film prints. Most of the cassettes were rented from The Wherehouse and Video Box in Northridge, California, but special mention must go to the following:
—Elaine Hoover and her friendly, helpful staff at Video West at 11372 Ventura Blvd., N. Hollywood, CA 91604, 818-760-0096. They had for rent or ordered for rent cassettes that were not available elsewhere.
—To Tim Wohlgemuth of Award Films for giving me a crash course on gay cinema by loaning me cassettes of important gay-themed films I might otherwise have overlooked.
—To Jerry Sole of New Yorker Films at 16 W. 61st St. in New York City for letting me view 16mm prints of Fassbinder films not on home video.
—To Bill Margold for letting me see cassettes of rarely available porn films.
—To Marga Aulback of AB Films for letting me view cassettes of a few of her porn productions at her office in Woodland Hills.
—And to Mike McClay of now-defunct VCX Video for letting me catch up on a variety of old and new porn films released by his company. The kindnesses of Margold and McClay in particular enabled me to see some important or interesting porn films I would otherwise have overlooked because there is too much porn in the world and too little of it that has any inherent erotic, dramatic or artistic merit.

The second, concurrent, phase involved a lot of input, advice and constructive criticism from friends, acquaintances and mass media professionals as to the tone, thrust, content and accuracy of various chapters. Without their help, this book would have been much different, less accurate and far less substantial in its text and visual content. General thanks go to Joan Anderson, Mistress Antoinette, Lloyd Drum, Garland Embrey, the late Mike Hodel, Jim Holliday, Hyapatia Lee, Dave Kiser, Kay Parker, Howard Prouty of the AFI library in Hollywood who assisted in preliminary title research, William Rotsler, Marc Sosniak, Arthur Tarlow and Kevin Thomas.

Special thanks go to:

—Marvin Jones and Tim Wohlgemuth for putting me on to a lot of important homosexual movies. Marvin was especially helpful in broadening my views of homosexual cinema, both pornographic and mainstream. His major professional complaint about gay porn is that "if gays are so sensitive and artistic, why can't they make a good porn movie?" Marvin also gave me some crucial insights for the teen exploitation chapter.

—Terry Hopwood of Family Synergy and Victims of Child Abuse Legislation (VOCAL). (It should be noted that these two organizations are entirely separate.) Terry is a charming, gracious, charismatic woman whose discussions with me about alternate family lifestyles—she has practiced open marriage since she was 18—opened my eyes and heart wide to the world beyond monogamy and caused me to virtually rewrite the chapter on adultery, making it richer in substance and ideas. She also gave me valuable input as to what was wrong with *Something About Amelia.* For those who want to find out more about Family Synergy, their address and phone number are POB 2668, Culver City, CA 90231, 818-765-5544; for those who want to find out more about VOCAL, their number is 714-547-5643.

—Bill Margold, whose editorial counseling on the porn chapter ensured its accuracy.

—And to the tireless, courteous, friendly staff of the Margaret Herrick Library of the Academy of Motion Picture Arts and Sciences in Beverly Hills. They were always there by phone to provide me with plot synopses, credits, release dates and production company information whenever I needed them.

The final phase was gathering all the illustrations. For this, general thanks go to the Academy, Aladdin Books in Fullerton, Peter H. Brown, Buelax Producciones, Cinema Collectors, Collector's Bookstore, Lisa Dixon, Patty Lombard and Laura Parker of Island Pictures, Larry Edmunds Cinema and Theatre Bookshop, Bette Gordon, Veronica Hart, Monica Heath of Caballero Home Video, Betty Johnson of Neptune Productions, Bruce Kimmel, Rick Lee, Harold Lime, Rika Mead of Leisure Time Ltd., Richard Milner, Paul Nagle of Catalina Productions, Roger Nau, Bill O'Connell of Almi Films, Kay Parker, Lynn Singer of USA Home Video, Evelyn Tecotsky of the MGM/UA legal department, Richard D. Thompson, Tim Wohlgemuth of Award Films, and Jane Wright of Spectrafilm.

Special thanks go to:

—Eddie Brandt's Saturday Matinee at 6310 Colfax Ave. in North Hollywood. Eddie's files contain thousands of choice stills and posters not available at other memorabilia stores. His shop is a friendly family store where obsessed movie buffs can feel right at home.

—Bill Margold, who let me have whatever I wanted from his huge collection of porno stills and slides, exploitation stills and horror and bondage film stills. Without his generous help, several chapters would have been visually lacking, especially the ones on kinky sex and pornography.

—Eric Hoffman, whose incredible collection of exploitation and porno posters and press books was a godsend.

—And Mike McClay of VCX Video, who let me choose what I wanted from his books of color slides and made black-and-white stills at his own expense especially for this book.

In addition to the various newspaper and magazine articles alluded to and discussed, and the investigative report on the Scott County, Minn., scandal loaned to me by Arthur Tarlow, my bibliography included three books and a magazine article:

—Parker Tyler's original volume on *Sex in Films* for Citadel Press.

—Vito Russo's *The Celluloid Closet: Homosexuality in the Movies* (Harper and Row, 1981), which is an entertainingly comprehensive look at the treatment of homosexuals in mainstream movies.

—Dan Schocket's "Reel Sex" article on the porno stardoms of Veronica Hart and Colleen Brennan in the July 1985 edition of *Penthouse Letters*. In this article, Schocket pinpoints with incisive enthusiasm what makes both women unique in porno movies and why they are two of the best and most erotic real actresses ever to appear in porn. He echoes my sentiments exactly, presenting an articulate precis on why these two dynamic women made a difference.

—And most of all, James L. Limbacher's two-volume masterwork *Sexuality in World Cinema* (Scarecrow Press, 1983). I especially recommend these books for Limbacher's splendid organization of research materials, and for his wit, humor, perceptions, guts, and breathtaking completeness of scope. This is not only an excellent reference work, it is delightful reading as well, though there are some omissions and inadvertent inaccuracies.

My biggest thanks of all go to Allan J. Wilson, editor-in-chief of Citadel Press, who approached me with this book and gave me the chance to prove myself in hardcover when no other publisher would. His gut feeling that I was the right man for the job gave me the big publishing break I desperately needed. He was a friendly, calm and fair taskmaster, and I hope I have the chance to work for and with him again.

Sam Frank
Los Angeles

The author gratefully acknowledges permission to quote from the following:

The Celluloid Closet: Homosexuality in the Movies (Harper & Row, 1981), by Vito Russo. Permission granted by Harper & Row and the author's agent.

"If All Men Were Brothers, Would You Let One Marry Your Sister?" copyright © 1968 by Theodore Sturgeon. Permission granted by Kirby McCauley, executor for the estate of Theodore Sturgeon.

Quote from the Family Synergy newsletter by permission of Terry Hopwood.

Quote from porn star Hyapatia Lee from a letter to the author dated March 1, 1985. This letter was written for the express purpose of being quoted in this book.

Quote from Terry Hopwood is from a phone conversation with the author in March of 1985.

Quote from porn star Kay Parker is from a phone conversation with the author in May of 1985.

Emmanuelle II: The
Joys of a Woman
(1975).

INTRODUCTION

I was just coming of age when sex became verbally and visually more explicit in American movies. Instead of the euphemistic pablum that used to pass for grown-up entertainment on screen, my adolescence saw the long overdue return of realism in stories, characters, dialogue and denouements. Movies no longer had to end happily to fit a pre-determined, mythical image of human behavior; they could now end the way the story dictated they should—which was a healthy and constructive move in the right direction. Tragedy can be uplifting too.

As I matured into young adulthood, I got my first whiffs of cinematic sexual freedom. *M*A*S*H* came along at just the right moment with its breezy, bawdy humor and anti-war irreverence; Ken Russell was electrifying with the bold bisexual eroticism and aesthetic pictorial schemes of *Women in Love* and *The Music Lovers;* John Schlesinger dealt honestly and poignantly with the worlds of homo- and bisexuality in *Sunday, Bloody Sunday,* while William Friedkin treated the emerging gay world as a limp-wristed, bitchy lark in *The Boys in the Band; Woodstock* celebrated the free love idealism of the hippie culture while Ralph Bakshi explored its cynical, street-wise underside in *Fritz the Cat;* Jack Nicholson epitomized both the stud mentality of an older generation caught up in self-destructive sexual conquest in *Carnal Knowledge,* and the identity crisis of the newer generation in *Five Easy Pieces;* Woody Allen made sexual neurosis comically cathartic in *Play it Again Sam;* Linda Lovelace made fellatio chic, fashionable and big box-office in *Deep Throat;* and *Myra Breckenridge* bewildered audiences with its sheer sexual perversity, though as a satire it was a heavily indulgent, jumbled misfire.

Clearly, the early 1970's were a time when American *and* British movies started growing up in their treatment of adult behavior and sexual dilemmas, covering as much ground in as little time as possible to make up for decades of censorship. But, for all the breakthroughs that were achieved, English-language films still had a way to go to achieve the level of wit and sophistication of the best American movies of the early 1930's before the Hays Code imposed a vise of moral hypocrisy and schizophrenia.

The newly devised rating system was supposed to liberate filmmakers to say and show what they wanted with few restrictions, but the system brought with it the same kind of Puritan hypocrisy that had conjured up the earlier movie code in the first place. The G rating meant there could be no dirty language or sexual content because it was intended for general or family films. Though there can certainly be powerful, uplifting films in this category, the G rating came to mean Disney and Muppet movies and other wholesome family fare.

The PG rating with its increasing levels of permissible violence caused the most dissension because it renewed the contention that ours is a society hypocritically worshipping violence over love. In PG, a few dirty words were allowed, as was passionate hugging and kissing, but no nudity and certainly no implicit sex. In R films, people could be shown fornicating and could use all kinds of so-called indecent language, but there was still a double standard governing nudity: women could expose themselves completely, but there could be no male crotch shots for fear of inviting ridicule of comparison. Even in highly touted X-rated films such as *Midnight Cowboy* (1969) and *Last Tango in Paris* (1973)—both of which were later re-rated to R—there was no exposure of male genitals. (The few male crotch shots that do exist in mainstream American movies are brief and incidental, Richard Gere being one of the few American stars to go frontal. Foreign filmmakers are far less prissy about male nudity and European film stars such as Gerard Depardieu have occasionally bared all.)

Eventually, the guidelines for these ratings were liberalized so that mere vulgarity wouldn't automatically earn an R, nor would softcore sex scenes garner an instant X. Movies like *Body Heat, Excalibur,* and *The Postman Always Rings Twice* that would have been rated X in the early 70's were given an R, whereas more explicit scenes of violence and sexual mayhem in *Scarface* and *Crimes of Passion* threatened to bring X back into the mainstream for the first time in years. Ironically, the first PG film to use the work "fuck" had nothing to do with sex. It was the excellent docudrama *All The President's Men* (1976), in which that word and other four-letter epithets are used in normal adult conversation.

In saying all of this, it should be remembered that the movie rating system is only a guideline and a voluntary one at that. It is *not* federal or state law nor has it ever been, though theater owners run the risk of being prosecuted for corrupting minors by selling them tickets to X-rated movies. Even the newly controversial PG-13—created as a result of the furor over *Indiana Jones and the Temple of Doom*—has no force of law and is intended only as a toothless warning to parents with impressionable children.

Though the rating system did enable directors of the 1970's to produce movies to compare with the best of Hollywood's Golden Age, the early years of the decade were mere baby steps compared to the real landmarks of the late 70's and early 80's. In fact, few of the movies summarized above are as fresh, innovative and provocative today as they seemed at the time. For all of the uncensored sexual expression, there is little that transcends what was clearly a transitional phase.

Compare those titles and their themes with these from the late 1970's to today: *Annie Hall,* the quintessential relationship movie of the 70's, *La Cage Aux Folles,* a soaring gay farce that makes *The Boys in the Band* look labored and amateurish; *Kiss of the Spiderwoman,* an incisively honest drama about cellmates who are political and sexual opposites but who find common ground in their mutual need for a trusting friendship; *Body Heat,* with its intricate noir plot and sizzling passion; *Centerfold Fever,* the porno equivalent of a Mel Brooks comedy and just as hilarious; *Roommates,* a landmark porno movie because of its exceptional production values for the genre, its erotic hardcore scenes, its sense of humor and its function as a showcase for the most talented woman ever to appear in porno, Veronica Hart; *Tootsie* and *Victor/Victoria,* rollicking comedies about role reversals that proved there is no substitute for solid, witty screenwriting and first-rate comic acting when you want to score satiric moral points; *Risky Business,* which proved that a movie about contemporary teenagers could have dimension and artistry and still appeal to the teen market; *The Grey Fox,* which marked a return to old-fashioned romantic sex with its love affair between a turn-of-the-century western bandit and a feminist photographer; and *Murphy's Romance,* which marked a welcome return to contemporary romantic courtship, showcasing in particular James Garner's easygoing charisma when we needed it most.

Just as the early sound films of the 1930's made a quantum leap in narrative quality when the technology improved and directors learned how to use the medium for more than just incessant talking, sex in cinema from the mid-1970's on became more than just an excuse to have people go through lascivious gyrations and agonies. It became more than an unrestricted license for rough language, kinky behavior and toilet humor for their own sake (there still is all of that in abundance and always will be in movies). It became a challenge to use the medium to reflect our evolving sexual reality by mirroring it from a variety of colorful facets and enlightening angles. Even though there has been a deluge of American movies in the last few years that make one ashamed to be a human being or make us look like sex-crazed retards—the stalk-and-slash horror movies and teen exploitation flicks respectively—other movies have come along to restore our faith in the powers of subtlety, humor and romance, and in the erotic punch of lovers cuddling in bed before *and* after intercourse.

Woody Allen has become our closest equivalent of Preston Sturges with his incisive and compassionate Jewish intellectual humor in movies like *Play it Again Sam, Annie Hall* and *The Purple Rose of Cairo;* Lawrence Kasdan with *Body Heat* has the makings of a Billy Wilder for the 80's, though he has come nowhere near the erotic punch of that movie in his later films; Blake Edwards brought back relaxed, polished, sophisticated sex comedy with *10, Victor/Victoria* and *Micki and Maude;* Ron Howard demonstrated *his* flair for offbeat romantic comedies with *Nightshift* and *Splash,* making him the heir apparent to Frank Capra, but slipped with the half-baked science-fiction notions of *Cocoon;* Rob Reiner displayed *his* flair for romantic sex comedy with the hilariously inspired *The Sure Thing;* Paul Bartel showed the makings of a master director of screwball comedy with the delightfully perverse *Eating Raoul;* Spain's Eloy de la Iglesia boldly combined Marxism with homosexual desire in *El Diputado* for a masterwork of class struggle within a sexual context; and Canada's John Sayles showed *his* genius with a poignant masterpiece of lesbian love called *Lianna.*

Perhaps most important of all, other movies have come along to alter our views of masculine/feminine sex appeal with male and female stars who did not fit the conventional commercial molds. We still have roguishly handsome stars like Paul Newman and Burt Reynolds, and hunks like John Travolta and Tom Selleck, but we also have plainer-looking sex symbols like Woody Allen, Dustin Hoffman and Dudley Moore. These are men who convey intelligence, humor and sensitivity, proving that brains are just as sexy as beefcake.

By the same token, our female stars are not all glamour queens. In fact, many of our top screen women are tomboyish beauties with inner strength and a great deal of emotional depth and fire. Actresses like Sally Field, Debra Winger, Margot Kidder, Sissy Spacek, Karen Allen, and Jill Clayburgh are as feisty as they are comforting, supportive of their men but equal to them in intelligence, guts, humor and romantic sensibility. It's a delight to watch these women take on the choicest female roles available, expanding their range and our collective consciousness.

In short, the best American, British and European films since 1970 have used sex in all its forms for mature, humane, humorously revealing commentaries on the sex we practice in real life, giving us a great deal to reflect on and dream about. And, just as the 1980's are going past mid-point, more fresh talents are coming along to probe even deeper, to turn our fears, hopes and fantasies inside-out on screen. For example, one of the hits of Filmex 84 in Los Angeles (which was released in 1985) was a film by director Bette Gordon called *Variety*, in which she honestly explored a young woman's sexual fantasies by keeping them human and out of the realm of feminist dogma.

One final, crucial development in this sexy saga is the explosive growth of the home video industry, enabling millions of people to watch most of the movies discussed in this book in the privacy of their homes. Ironically, many good movies that fail at the box-office are bestsellers on home video, ensuring that a number of neglected masterworks get seen by a wide audience. But, for all the comfort and inexpensiveness of seeing new and old movies at home, there is still nothing to compare with seeing a beautifully made, well-told film story on the big screen where it belongs. A lot of movies lose their impact on the home screen. Still, home video has become the entertainment wave of the future, chomping big chunks out of the theatrical box office, and doubtless those bites will get larger in the next few years.

This introduction is intended to summarize what the following chapters will explore in greater detail through text and pictures. How the unfettered sexual cinema has evolved since 1970, and the kinds of experiences we might be looking forward to in the next 10 to 15 years. If memories are evoked and feelings are stirred, so much the better.

Read on and enjoy.

Chapter I
HIPPIES & SWINGERS

"Free love was not just a slogan for the hippies, it was a way of life, a means of reaching out physically and emotionally to shatter the middle-class bonds of sexual hypocrisy and insecurity. The shame of it was that the word "hippy" caught on and came to mean in essence a dirty, long-haired bum, and that Hollywood movies never treated seriously the emotional and philosophical inner core of the "hippy" movement."

—Anonymous quote from an old magazine article.

"Swinging is a way of sharing sexual pleasure with new friends and of strengthening emotional bonds with old friends. For a couple to tell each other it's okay to make love to someone else is to express the utmost confidence in their relationship as a couple. It sure beats the hell out of jealousy and sneaking around the corner for extra sex."

—From a panel discussion at a swingers' seminar.

When the Hays Code was finally and unlamentably abolished in 1966, and with it the Breen Office which enforced that Code, the timing couldn't have been better. The radical youth or hippie movement with its emphasis on "free love" was at its peak, while the mate-swapping or swinging culture was on the rise. Naturally, Hollywood studios were eager to capitalize on these hot sexual trends and to do so without having to tapdance around provocative themes.

The movies that resulted from the hippie and swinger phenomena were both candid and exploitational, sometimes even honest, occasionally erotic. The effect on the American public, at least for a few years, was intoxicating, and the long box-office lines around the country encouraged Hollywood and foreign filmmakers to keep going further until every taboo was shattered in the name of commerce. Sex didn't just sell tickets, it became a major thrust (pun intended) of commercial moviemaking. Not that this

produced many lasting works of art or sheer entertainment, but at least the movies were able to rediscover their sex organs even if it was only to masturbate them until they learned how to make love with them.

The movies that focused on so-called "hippies" generally emphasized media stereotypes, often the more superficial or negative aspects of those stereotypes such as drug dealing or living like a raggedy bum in a commune or one-room bohemian hovel surrounded by hip posters and books. Let's not forget, though, that the term "hippie" was a media contrivance, a derogatory catch-word to denote teenagers and young adults who were part of an anti-establishment "hip culture." Unlike most movie versions, a real hippy was someone who was anti-war, specifically the war in Vietnam; who was against the rape of the environment by oil and lumber companies; who rebelled against conventional middle-class values such as monogamy and an office job; who espoused and practiced guiltless pre-marital sex and communal marriage as a means of shedding our outmoded Puritan heritage; and who advocated wide-sweeping, radical political changes as the only means of transforming for the better a sick bourgeois society obsessed with militarism, crass commercialism and property rights over human rights.

The physical emblems of the hippies were long hair and beards on men (the hair especially being a primary symbol of rebellious independence), marijuana cigarettes, blue jeans, colorful T-shirts, love beads, head bands, psychedelic art, and guitars for playing folk songs and rock music. Other, more fundamental facets of the hippy lifestyle included the legendary love-ins and be-ins which emphasized spiritual consciousness and free or unpossessive sexual love. These external and internal values were celebrated on stage as The Age of Aquarius in the rock musical *Hair,* and on film in Michael Wadleigh's documentary of the 1969 Woodstock rock music festival in upstate New York.

By the time *Hair* finally reached the screen in 1979, even a gifted director like Milos Forman could not recapture the original experience, could not give it compelling shape as a film event except for a few chilling scenes. The play seemed horribly dated and more of a clichéd artifact than a passionately meaningful evocation of a turbulent and exciting period in American history. The sexual freedoms shown openly on stage (remember, this *was* the first major American play featuring total nudity, though it wasn't at all prurient) and the vulgar, profane language considered so shocking in the late 1960's were taken for granted a decade later.

Woodstock (1970) didn't suffer from any such trivialization because it was the real article: a verité, stereophonic recapturing of a pivotal musical event released less than a year after that event, and which gave us the phrase "the Woodstock nation" (though the concert didn't take place *at* Woodstock, only nearby) because this unprecedented gathering of half a million young people seemed to demonstrate in one showing that the values of peace and love and rock 'n' roll espoused by the hippies *could* work *en masse.* The movie is still brilliantly evocative—especially in a theater with the sound turned up full blast—and the rock acts and offstage couplings still convey audiovisual excitement, but the event itself had little long-term social impact. All it really proved was that a large number of young Americans could gather to screw, smoke pot and listen to rock music for three days without murdering each other.

In 1969, the Woodstock festival was viewed as the apotheosis of American hip music culture. In these scenes from the 1970 documentary of that event, hip youths are seen sitting around in the nude or wading into a stream…

…while others take a much-needed shower break during three days of rock and folk music celebration.

The hippie dream of peace and love became a shattered illusion when battalions of riot cops violently broke up anti-war college sit-ins like the one fictionalized in The Strawberry Statement (1970).

Opportunistic Fritz the Cat happily cops a feel from a hippie student in Fritz the Cat *(1972).*

But is clearly annoyed when a bunch of doped-out hippies move in on his sexual preserve.

Less idyllic were college movies like *The Strawberry Statement* (1970), which dealt with the love affair of a politcally uncommitted young student (Bruce Davison) and a campus activist (Kim Darby) within the context of the Columbia University riots of the late 60's. What little importance this movie has as a chunk of its era derives more from the visceral power of the sit-in demonstration sequence than from the evolving sexual partnership of Davison and Darby. The nightsticks used by a battalion of goonish head-beating cops are far more phallic than anything else in the movie, potently symbolizing fascist suppression of civil disobedience.

Violence was also at the heart of *Joe* (1970) and *Billy Jack* (1971). In *Joe* (which has a drug-dealing hippie as the catalyst), bigoted blue-collar worker Peter Boyle railed obscenely against blacks, welfare workers and hippies, ended up having sex with a doped-out hippie chick for the adulterous thrill of it, then blew away several other hippies with a shotgun in the self-righteous belief that "the world is better off without those scum." These acts make Boyle a murderous hypocrite, driving home the movie's contrived melodramatic point that self-styled "patriots" like Joe are nothing more than opportunistic thugs, ready to kill anyone who threatens their middle-class status quo.

Billy Jack, on the other hand, seemed to embody all of the cultural and spiritual values advocated by the counterculture, including free love. At the time, it seemed to be an excitingly realistic dramatization of the clash between hypocritical establishment authorities and mentally "together" youngsters living at a communal free school. It was *the* hippie movie of the 70's. All it looks like today is an amateurishly acted string of melodramatic clichés and banal political generalities about freedom vs. oppression, with a gratuitous rape thrown in for good manipulative measure. Tom Laughlin's Billy Jack is meant to be a messianic populist folk hero, but he is nothing more than a proverbial western loner who uses karate instead of a gun to put the local rednecks in their place. Violence in the name of peace.

One actress who personified the hippie image both on- and offscreen was Barbara Hershey. She got paid to be a surrogate womb for a childless middle-class couple in *The Baby Maker* (1970) on the assumption that a hippie woman is more open sexually to that sort of thing; she helped her contentious lover escape the law on a manslaughter charge in *The Pursuit of Happiness* (1971); and ran drugs with a renegade lover in *Dealing: or the Berkeley-to-Boston Forty-Brick Lost Bag Blues* (1972). She was a sexual free spirit in these movies, ranging in characterization from shrewd

pluckiness to the dippier aspects of the hippie mentality; a goofy sort of all-embracing love that was vacuously childlike. In *The Baby Maker,* this sexual naiveté gave way for a couple of reels to a maturing outlook as Hershey became emotionally involved with father-to-be Sam Groom, overreacted to the unreasoning jealousy and resulting infidelity of spaced-out boyfriend Scott Glenn (for a free-wheeling hippie girl, she is remarkably angry when her lover practices the free love she spends most of the movie vigorously espousing), and came to term with child. She seemed to grow up real fast, dealing unhappily with real emotions instead of the slogan type, but in the end she reverts to stereotype, shrugging off the ordeal as a mere "happening" that netted her some extra cash. In essence, *The Baby Maker* is a dull, pretentious, hypocritical product of its time.

The most vacuous hippie chick of them all was Leigh Taylor-Young in the satiric *I Love You Alice B. Toklas* (1968). Though it's a pre-1970 movie, it has to be mentioned because it poked hilarious fun at many of the "far-out" pretensions of the hippie culture, in particular "dropping out to find yourself." Its importance to this discussion is that Taylor-Young's flower child is an uncritical, blindly accepting fantasy caricature who gives free sexual love to straight Jewish lawyer turned hippie Peter Sellers so long as he doesn't expect or demand commitment; her love is open to all comers, especially other spaced-out bubblebrains.

The funniest and most humane of all the hippie-themed movies was Milos Forman's fresh-eyed, generation-gap satire *Taking Off* (1971), which took a warmly objective view of fluctuating American sexual mores. He doesn't take sides in his story of a square

Campus activists Bruce Davison and Kim Darby snatch a moment of non-political passion in between radical activities in The Strawberry Statement *(1970).*

Far-out lawyer-turned-hippie Peter Sellers enjoys a tender moment with spaced-out Leigh Taylor-Young in I Love You Alice B. Toklas *(1968).*

Hippie chick Barbara Hershey (left) gets paid by middle-class couple Sam Groom and Colin Wilcox-Horne to be a surrogate womb for them in The Baby Maker *(1970).*

But the growing closeness between Hershey and Groom causes some anxious bedtime moments for the now familial threesome.

middle-class couple (Buck Henry and Lynn Carlin) searching for their runaway teen daughter (Linnea Heacock) in bohemian Greenwich Village, but seeks to understand the concerns on both sides. In essence, he is saying that we are all responsible for the lack of communication between parents and children, but that a freeing of one's sexual views to promote that communication does not give one license to act like a fool. Coupled with *I Love You Alice B. Toklas, Taking Off* put the hippie counterculture in fine comic perspective while marking the beginning of the gradual demise of hippie movies as a commercial genre.

At the same time hippies were having their brief moment in American life and movies, the swinging movement was capturing other imaginations with its bold license to indulge in carnal pleasure for its own sake through uninhibited, unjealous mate-swapping. However, swinging is not to be confused with open or group marriage because, while swinging can involve open marriage, it generally stresses sexual adventures with as many people as possible, either one-on-one or in groups. Open marriages focus on consistent, meaningful relationships in terms of primary and secondary relationships, while group contracts go further by expanding the conventional nuclear family to a mutu-

ally committed adult trio or group of couples. All of these lifestyles have their merits and advantages because they encourage guiltless extramarital sexual intimacy and friendship.

Swinging in particular can channel pure lust in a direct and immediately gratifying way. And it's a movement that's on the rise. Look through any swinger magazine at today's newsstands and you will discover swing clubs and swinger contact services by the score nationwide. Most are your average clubhouses or orgy groups, while others cater to specialized needs. Some, like *The Hung Jury, The White Boys' Auxiliary* and *The Gentlemen 7,* are underground, depending on word-of-mouth for membership. *The Hung Jury* is a Los Angeles-based national club catering to single and married women seeking well-endowed lovers of any race; *The White Boys' Auxiliary* is an informal east coast network of married white men seeking well-hung black lovers for their size queen wives; and *The Gentlemen 7* (actually *15* men) is an elite east coast clique of professional men servicing married women in their spare time, but only with their husbands' consent.

When the swinging movement began in earnest in the U.S. in the mid to late 60's, it was mainly a fledgling core of white couples interested in straight-forward sex with other white couples. In the last ten years, though, judging by all the swinging magazines, five trends have emerged as primary among swingers:

1) the search for well-endowed men of any race by single and married women, but especially blacks for white women because the myth lives on that black men are bigger, better, more virile lovers than white men; 2) female bisexuality; 3) sex with animals; 4) scatalogical sex (urination and defecation); and 5) domination games. Sadomasochism has become an important part of the swing scene for a growing number of swingers, though it is still a fringe movement.

However, you won't see any of this reflected either in late 60's-early 70's movies about swingers, or in any contemporary American movies except for porno films and a delightful satire called *Eating Raoul,* about which more later on. The handful of mainstream swinger movies ranged from Paul Mazursky's ground-breaking *Bob & Carol & Ted & Alice* (1969) to the drab 1977 documentary *Sandstone.*

At the time, *Bob & Carol & Ted & Alice* seemed a boldly seriocomic exploration of alternate lifestyles, with Robert Culp and Natalie Wood cheerfully con-verting best friends Elliott Gould and Dyan Cannon to the joys of mate-swapping. The experiment ended in awkward disaster, proving, at least in Mazursky's eyes, that swinging is not a viable route to sexual freedom.

Hippie wanderer Laure Bird gives nomadic race car driver James Taylor a good-luck kiss in Two-Lane Blacktop *(1971).*

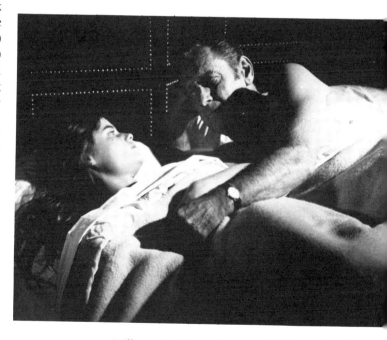

William Holden in Breezy *(1973) is clearly worried about the rightness of his affair with hippie teen Kay Lenz.*

Radley Metzger's *The Lickerish Quartet* (1970) disagreed, but did so by playing pretentious illusion vs. reality games with the audience. When a group of libertines run across an actress from a porn film in their collection, they show her the movie but she isn't in it, someone else is, then they themselves are, and thus the movie goes on in tail-chasing fashion, trying to be hip and arty but failing to be even a turn-on.

Claude Berri's *Le Sex Shop* (1973) was a more honest and comically healthy look at both the swinging phenomenon and our increasing preoccupation with sex. As a failed bookstore owner who turns to selling porn, Berri becomes the kid in his own erotic candy shop, turned on to the idea of making love outside his marriage, but inhibited from doing so; partly because of moral conditioning, partly because the reality proves to be less appealing than the fantasy, partly because the only woman he really wants to be with is his wife. Which is the way a lot of people flirt with swinging; they see it as their ticket to sexual nirvana with no obligations other than to have a good time. But, when it comes to actual performance, either the single guy can't get it up, or in the couple's case it's for the husband's sake and the wife is fuming with jealousy, or they are both petrified with fright. Swinging is not for everyone.

In porn movies, though, swinging is *de rigueur,* and the action is always heavy. In movies like *Resurrection of Eve* (1973), *Taboo* (1980), *Taboo II* (1981) and *Plato's the Movie* (1980), the camera is everywhere, lingering over all the writhing couples. But some porn movies, like *Taboo II,* give orgies a bad name by showing swingers who look bored or blasé. If it's that much of a chore, why bother?

And then there is *Eating Raoul* (1982), Paul Bartel's delightfully offbeat satire on swingers, perverts and sadomasochists. He and Mary Woronov play asexual marrieds Paul and Mary Bland who come up with an ingenious scheme for raising money to buy their dream restaurant (Paul is a gourmet cook): lure swingers and perverts to their apartment with the promise of kinky sex, kill them with a bop on the head from a frying pan and relieve them of the extraordinary amounts of money they're carrying as pocket change. They hit the jackpot at a swinging party when Paul murders the whole lot of them with a single deft maneuver.

The whole purpose of *Eating Raoul* is to make affectionate fun of all the kinkos who inhabit Hollyweird, and it succeeds beautifully, though you do wonder why it is that no one asks what happened to all the victims.

Straight swinging on film had its last American gasp in 1977 with *Looking for Mr. Goodbar* and *Sandstone,* and it is interesting to contrast the two. *Looking for Mr. Goodbar* purports to be a sociological study of a schizoid personality, that of a woman (Diane Keaton) brought up in a tyrannically Catholic household who is a teacher by day and a bar cruiser by night, indiscriminately taking home all kinds of flakes and weirdos. Eventually, she is stabbed to death by a psychopathic stud (Tom Berenger) who is freaking out over his homosexuality. The lesson is supposed to be that swinging courts danger and death, but the incident that brings about Keaton's murder is a convenient contrivance and, anyway, the real crux of the movie is what motivates her to be a swinger in the first place. We are supposed to infer it's because she's rebelling against her father (Richard Kiley), but this is too pat and easy. All we do learn is that she enjoys her double life and is an easy lay. Some psychology.

Sandstone, though, is a verité look at the now defunct Malibu swinger's retreat founded by John and Barbara Williamson. There is nothing sensationalistic about this film, but nothing appealing either because the approach is too low-key and because the swingers we see are a humorless group, given to pretentious platitudes and self-righteous explications about the higher consciousness that comes with swinging. All that double-talk aside, Sandstone was a sex club, pure and simple, and it's doubtful that anyone became more highly "evolved" as a result of going there.

The swinging we do see at Sandstone is not very titillating either; mainly a lot of couples humping on mats laid side-by-side, trying desperately to reach orgasm. No one talks while making love, no one gets romantically intimate, it's all single-minded screwing. Which is what swinging is mainly all about. But, it's no fun watching it on screen, especially when you don't give a damn about the people doing it.

Diane Keaton easily and willingly succumbs to Richard Gere's sleazy charm in Looking for Mr. Goodbar. *(1977).*

Swinger Peter Sellers appears to be having difficulty undressing his latest chippy, Goldie Hawn, in There's a Girl in My Soup *(1974).*

In Erotic Aerobics *(1984), basic calisthenics
in a barn are just an excuse for orgiastic
groupings, including a twosome (fore-
ground) and threesome (background).*

So, except for occasional porn features, swinging
is not seen in contemporary American movies, which
may be just as well, but you'd think someone would
get the idea of conjuring a sizzling drama dealing with
the various emotional and sexual conflicts and crises
that come with the territory, to examine how all kinds
of people evolve into this lifestyle with ease and
comfort while others shy away from it. Hollywood, of
course, is scared of touching the subject.

Looking at the alternative lifestyles represented
by hippies and swingers, we can see that the hippie
legacy as reflected in movies was, overall, a negative
one, mainly drugs and pretentious language. And yet,
real-life hippies defected back to their middle-class
environs after a few years in communes, some of them
becoming part of the socio-political system they had
fought against, hoping to change it from within, which
they did to some extent, some more liberally than
others. Now instead of hippies we have yuppies (an
equally derogatory term), who are single-mindedly
obsessed with materialistic goals.

The swinging legacy, though, has been an ongoing one, but not at the movies; it's too hot to handle.
Nevertheless, swinging is gaining in popularity if not
in mainstream acceptability as the perfect, normal
outlet for an active, healthy libido. It can certainly be a
lot of fun if you have the drive and temperament for it.

To each his own.

Chapter 2
GAYS AND BISEXUALS

"As expressed on screen, America was a dream that had no room for the existence of homosexuals. Laws were made against depicting such things on screen. And when the fact of our existence became unavoidable, we were reflected, on screen and off, as dirty secrets."— From *The Celluloid Closet: Homosexuality in the Movies by* Vito Russo.

Judge: Is it true that you·are suffering from sexual perversion?
Quentin Crisp: It *is* true that I am a sexual pervert, but I don't know that I am suffering from it.—From *The Naked Civil Servant*

As with all previously forbidden subjects, once the Hays/Breen Code was abolished in the late 1960's, homosexuality came out of the celluloid closet, announcing itself for what it is: a sexual preference that is simply different from the heterosexual norm. Not an illness or a disease or a form of contagious sexual plague, but a desire to be with one's own sex that is as deep-rooted in the human race as the more traditional male-female urges. The honest movies depicting homosexual life, especially those made since 1975, have been healthy for their frankness, humanity and long overdue insights, and aggravating for their corruption of the English language.

For one thing, unless you qualify yourself in speaking or writing, you cannot use the word "gay" any more in its original meanings of merry or lively. And the phrase "gays and lesbians" is plainly redundant because lesbians are *de facto* gay. For that reason, the title of this chapter implies both sexes.

The gay-themed American and foreign films of the late 1960's through mid-1970's were a mixed lot, the result of a timid entertainment industry unused to dealing with a previously hidden minority it deemed loathsome except in terms of clichés. Major directors turned out major movies ranging from the blatantly stereotypical to the poetically artful, all of them bearing the initial cultural shock of unabashed homosexual friendship and love, often portrayed by established straight actors.

Hollywood's breakthrough film was William Friedkin's adaptation of Mart Crowley's bitchy birthday party comedy *The Boys in the Band* (1970), a gay *Who's Afraid of Virginia Woolf?* conjuring up almost every homosexual stereotype—along with a couple of normal-sounding characters—while pretending to deal seriously with the gay life. Homosexual audiences took all the agonizing over being gay and lost and found loves to heart because it was the only major

Tim Curry as Dr. Frank N. Furter in The
Rocky Horror Picture Show *(1975) struts his
stuff in outrageously campy style...*

movie in town recognizing their existence as feeling individuals, but that made the movie no less offensive for its patronizing attitude.

Friedkin followed it in 1980 with the even more revoltingly stereotypical *Cruising,* purporting to depict the gay leather bar scene in Manhattan, but twisting the reality of that underground culture into a brutalistic nightmare. Friedkin is clearly a director who views gay males as either laughably guilt-plagued queens or as hard, tough, butch bully boys; men who are innately neurotic or violent precisely because they are homosexual. This is like saying that heterosexuals are innately neurotic or violent because they're straight. And yet *Cruising* easily got studio backing because Friedkin was a commercial name, whereas Ron Peck and Paul Hallam in England spent three years getting *Nighthawks* (1978) financed so that they could depict the gay bar syndrome from a gay viewpoint. West Germany's Frank Riploh had to personally finance his low-budget *Taxi Zum Klo (Taxi to the Toilet,* 1981), which depicted the toilet room aspect of the cruising scene. Only French director Patrice Chereau apparently had an easier time of getting financing for his *L'Homme Blesse (The Wounded Man,* 1984), a bleak study of the ugly world of train depot hustling and pickups in France. All three films were critically acclaimed by straight and gay critics, though straight viewers are likely to leave (or walk out on) *Taxi Zum Klo* and *L'Homme Blesse* feeling exceptionally dirty. Riploh's film has an honestly raw feel to it, while Chereau's, for all its professional realism, lacks character motivations and insights. The former is merely sordid while the latter relentlessly drags your mind through the gutter. Each is an ordeal to sit through.

Another cliché of gay life is that homosexuals are innately sensitive artists. That message came through obliquely in Luchino Visconti's *Death in Venice* (1971), in which Dirk Bogarde as a Mahler-like composer is literally obsessed to death with a beautiful young boy. It came through loud and clear in Ken Russell's *The Music Lovers* (1971), one of the damndest biographical movies ever made. An exhilarating if highly inaccurate Freudian fantasy on the life of Tchaikovsky (brilliantly played by Richard Chamberlin), it attempts to connect the composer's homosexuality with his prolific output and the types of music he composed. This begs the question of whether one needs to be effeminate to be sensitive—of course not—or if Tchaikovsky was simply a great composer—which he was—who happened to be homosexual.

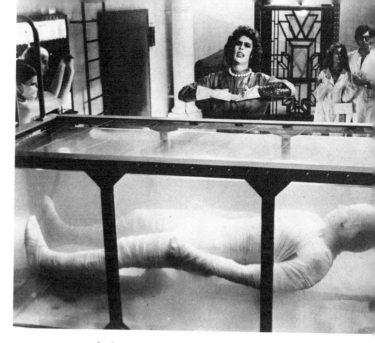

...before attending to the serious work of creating his very own he-man Adonis. Straight couple Susan Sarandon and Barry Bostwick in the background are later happily seduced by Curry. (Courtesy Landmark Theatres)

In the distortive Cruising *(1980), homicide cop Al Pacino danced his way into the gay leather bar scene in hope of finding a psychopathic gay killer.*

West Germany's Frank Riploh (right) more honestly documented the cruising scene he knew in Taxi Zum Kloh *(1981), here getting chummy with a fellow Halloween partygoer. (Courtesy Landmark Theatres)*

The BBC broke its own gay ban with The Naked Civil Servant *(1975), starring John Hurt (right) as real-life homosexual Quentin Crisp (left).*

John Hurt as Quentin Crisp in The Naked Civil Servant.

Christopher Gable (right) fears he might be losing composer lover Richard Chamberlain (as Tchaikovsky) in The Music Lovers *(1971).*

Ironically, two of the best gay-themed films of the early 70's were TV movies: *That Certain Summer* (1972) and *The Naked Civil Servant* (1975), both landmark movies in that they dealt with homosexuality honestly and without false sentiment. The first film, with its story of two mature professional men (Hal Holbrook and Martin Sheen) who happen to be lovers, confronted the mass TV audience with the simple truth that homosexual males are not all fluttering queens, that they can be just as straight in demeanor as heterosexuals. Though Holbrook's climactic speech to his son, Scott Jacoby, was a cop-out forced on the writers by ABC censors, *That Certain Summer* remains a model of how to eloquently dramatize a previously taboo subject without sensationalizing it.

Thames Television soared even higher with the biographical *The Naked Civil Servant,* the story of self-proclaimed effeminate homosexual Quentin Crisp (superbly played by John Hurt), whose life was dedicated to breaking the homophobic stranglehold of British society from the late 1920's onward. Indeed, *The Naked Civil Servant* is not so much about being homosexual as it is about the right to be different. It is also a rare instance of a performance in which we see the main character as he sees himself: a polite but flamboyant noncomformist who crusades against impossible cultural odds. For once, the usually comic image of the swishy gay is used as the foundation for a deeply affecting characterization. After a while, you cease thinking of Crisp in sexual terms, seeing him only as a man whose innate kindliness and compassion endear him to hundreds of people, both straight and gay. His story is ultimately a sad one, but makes the profound moral point that homosexuals have no less dignity and worth as people than do heterosexuals simply because they *are* homosexual.

At the same time homosexuals were finally being given screen time to state their case dramatically, bisexuals were having a field day, and a strange one at that. For some reason, most movies from 1970 to 1975 featuring a bisexual character implied that such people are innately decadent and amoral, often quick and eager to manipulate and murder, either to prevent exposure of criminality or to climb the social ladder. Handsome blond Peter McEnery in *Entertaining Mr. Sloan* and suave Michael York in *Something for Everyone* (both 1970) both used their charming switchability as weapons for deceit and murder to attain a cushy, pampered existence; and would-be De Gaulle assassin Edward Fox in *The Day of the Jackal* (1973) had no compunction about murdering both male and female lovers once they learned who and what he really was.

The most erotically decadent bisexual of the lot—and the most fun—was easily Tim Curry as Dr. Frank N. Furter, the sashaying "transvestite from transexual Transylvania" in the wonderfully weird cult classic *The Rocky Horror Picture Show* (1975). Here is perverse switch-hitting with campy style as Curry playfully seduces straight arrow Barry Bostwick and his fianceé Susan Sarandon.

One of the few *non*-decadent bisexuals was Murray Head in John Schlesinger's sleeper drama, *Sunday, Bloody Sunday* (1971), carrying on with gay Peter Finch and straight Glenda Jackson. This is one of the few mainstream movies yet made which depicts bisexuality as a matter-of-fact alternative rather than as a momentary diversion or aberrational lapse best and quickly forgotten. And yet, *Sunday, Bloody Sunday* is not so much about sexual lifestyles as it is about two people involved with the same man who cannot get him to commit on a permanent basis to one or the other of them. So they spend the entire movie engaged in a sexual tug of war. This sounds more compelling and provocative than it is because the truth is that this is one of Schlesinger's least effective films. The problems are overly quiet pacing and direction and a colorless performance by Head, making you wonder what Finch and Jackson see in him. With a more charismatic actor in the lead and more forceful direction by Schlesinger, *Sunday, Bloody Sunday* could have been a memorable movie beyond the then-shocking sight of Finch and Head passionately kissing.

Another recurring, popular theme in gay films is homosexuality in private schools, usually Catholic ones. Examples from the 1960's include the recently rediscovered *This Special Friendship* (1964) and *If ...* (1969). The most popular film of this type in the last ten years is the Danish *You Are Not Alone* (1978), focusing on two pre-teen boys expressing innocently physical boyish affection at a boarding school in

In the landmark American TV movie, That Certain Summer *(1972), homosexual love was depicted with sympathetic seriousness. Here, Scott Jacoby is literally caught in the middle between dad Hal Holbrook (right) and his dad's lover, Martin Sheen.*

Denmark. It is the bestselling video title for Award Films and its popularity is understandable because it has moments of Truffaut-like candor, sweetness and naturalism that diffuse any moral objections to its subject. A particularly tender scene is shown here.

A more historical film in this genre is *Another Country* (1983), based on the true story of Guy Burgess and his repressed homosexual yearnings at Oxford in the early 1930's. The movie's tone is deliberately as stiff-upper-lip as the class structure it depicts, evoking a bygone era of cruel sexual behavior and rigid male behavior codes.

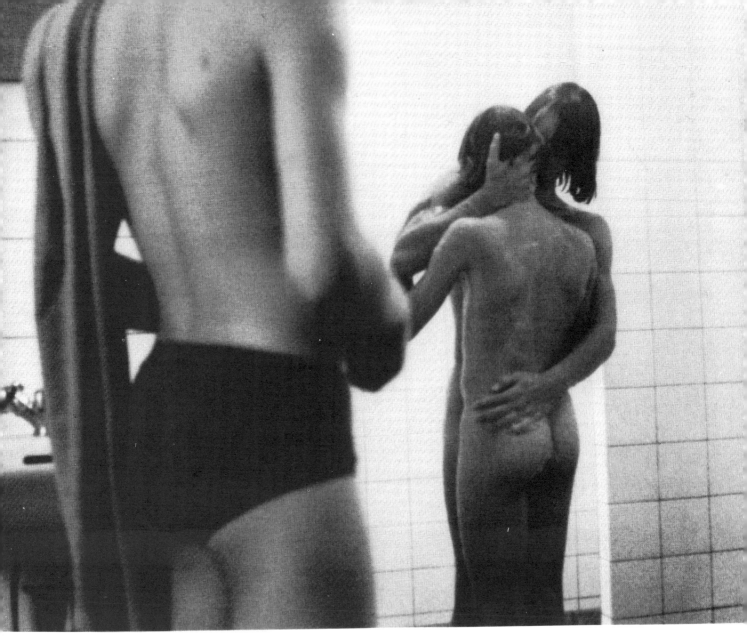

Boyish friendship could also blossom into tender physical affection as seen here in the Danish film You Are Not Alone *(1978).*

Two other boyfriends in that film share a quiet, happy moment in the woods. (Courtesy Award Films)

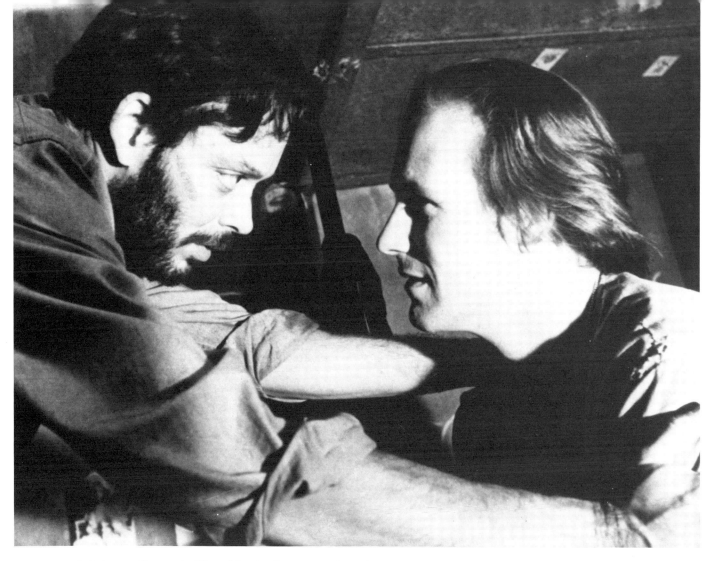

As prison cellmates in Kiss of the Spiderwoman *(1985), straight Raul Julia (left) and gay William Hurt embrace in friendship and physical love. (Courtesy Island Pictures)*

Yet another theme is corruption of the young, exemplified by Salvatore Semperi's *Ernesto* (1979), and Hector Babenco's *Pixote* (1981). *Ernesto* is a carefully crafted study of emotional callousness in which a teenage clerk (Martin Halm) is seduced by a sensitive dockworker (Michele Placido) and uses his newly awakened homosexual feelings to use people for smugly self-assured ends. *Pixote* is a gorgeously photographed, unsparing look at juvenile delinquency in Brazil in which one of the young hoodlums is a semi-transvestite homosexual. However, his homosexuality is not a symptom of his environment but part of his nature, thriving on the pent-up urges of the other young thieves.

In *Kiss of the Spiderwoman* (1985), Babenco returned to a prison environment, this time with a different fix on homosexual love. The focus is on two cellmates in an unnamed foreign country. One is a self-absorbed, heterosexual Marxist (Raul Julia) who views life in terms of revolutionary dogma, not human attachments. The other is an effeminate, transvestite gay (William Hurt) who loves kitschy movies and who passes their time recounting in lurid detail the plot of a melodramatic Nazi propaganda film about honor, duty and betrayal. As the film-within-a-film unfolds (starring Sonia Braga as a highly exaggerated femme fatale), we see that it is intended as a parable on the relationship between Julia and Hurt, the former living his life as all cause, the latter as all unquestioning feeling.

Gradually, these men draw together in common human bond, the gay helping the straight in his hours of physical need: medically, emotionally and finally sexually. The point of conflict is that Hurt is bribed by prison officials with early parole to get Julia to reveal information about his Marxist gang, but in the end he cannot do that because he has fallen in love with the man and almost vice-versa. Homophobia turns to

Margit Carstensen as the title character of Fassbinder's The Bitter Tears of Petra von Kant *(1973) reclines in bed brooding over her lesbian lover. The half-smiles here are as close to human as this movie gets. Tableaus are all that matter. (Courtesy New Yorker Films)*

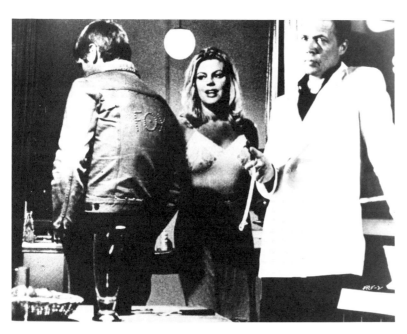

In the title role of his Fox and His Friends *(1975), writer/director Rainer Werner Fassbinder as a lower class bum is not doing too well with a more elite gay chum.*

genuine affection for a fellow man regardless of sexual preference while opportunism erodes into the age-old choice between betraying your friend or your country. What makes this resonate is that Babenco, a homosexual, subtly underscores the notion that human need is blind to labels of straight and gay. Thus, when Julia and Hurt finally do make love, it is not shocking so much as inevitable. The movie works as well as it does as a moving drama of pretension vs. humanity because of the lead performances, especially Hurt's. His is the showier role but because of that he has the chance to take risks, to gradually and subtly devolve from studied gay theatricality to unguarded straightforward concern for the well-being of another. Both *Pixote* and *Kiss of the Spider Woman* are alike in that regard; their homosexual characters are both deeply caring souls behind their effeminate facades.

Compare those two movies to the gay-themed films of another highly acclaimed director: West Germany's Rainer Werner Fassbinder. He emerged in the late 1960's as an acclaimed wunderkind who used gay subjects to realistically explore psychological and class struggles. He was prolific to say the least, but overrated based on the films I've seen.

The Bitter Tears of Petra von Kant (1973), *Fox and His Friends* (1975), *In a Year of 13 Moons* (1976) and *Querelle* (1983) are such a dismal lot I have to wonder whence the praise. The first film aroused lesbian ire because the title and ad campaign implied a negative theme. It's about a lesbian slumber party set in a single room that amounts to nothing more than the title character and her associates yakking incessantly and monotonally about her failed marriage and their dull lives. You wonder why Fassbinder didn't show what they are talking about. Was his budget so low he could only afford to have these boring women sit around in recitative tableaus?

In a Year of 13 Moons is even worse. A lonely transexual (Volker Spengler) gets into a screaming fight with her lover, then bemoans her fate to a female friend while they tour a slaughterhouse. For a full ten minutes, we are treated to the revolting death symbolism of bulls being bled and butchered. The movie goes downhill from there, ending with Spengler's death.

Worst of all is Fassbinder's final film, the atrocious *Querelle,* in which sailor Brad Davis learns the painful pleasure of anal sex with a macho brothel owner. The lugubrious narrator tells us what the movie should be showing us—mystical rubbish about Querelle's inner nature—while Fassbinder tries to elevate the tone of this trash with choir music and a symbolic fantasy scene straight out of the Passion of Christ.

Fox and His Friends is the only relatively entertaining film of the four, but the story is so predictable

Macho gangster James Garner is disturbed by his attraction to female impersonator Julie Andrews in Victor/Victoria *(1982) because his masculine pride won't let him concede anything other than heterosexual attractions.*

you wonder why Fassbinder bothered. He plays the title role, a homely, unskilled circus bum who wins a lottery and is fleeced for the money by his unscrupulous upper-class lover. The manipulation is obvious, and the abandonment by the lover is inevitable, as is Fox's suicide—so for all the competent craftsmanship and arty staging, it's hard to give a damn.

A far more sophisticated director of homosexual themes and characters is Blake Edwards with *10* (1979), *S.O.B.* and *Victor/Victoria* (both 1982). In *10*, Robert Webber is Dudley Moore's scabrously menopausal songwriting partner, a man who uses caustic humor as a cover for a shallow relationship with a handsome young beach bum, revealing a depth of feeling when the young man leaves him.

Even better is Robert Preston in the other two films, first as a gay hairdresser in *S.O.B.*, then his soaring triumph as the blithe cabaret performer in *Victor/Victoria* who persuades Julie Andrews to become a female impersonator (q.v. also chapter on Drag Queens and Role Reversals). Preston steals the show with his relaxed affability, making you wish all *straight* men were this charmingly congenial.

Edwards makes a further statement about alternate sexuality with the mobster and bodyguard characters played by James Garner and Alex Karras.

Garner is distressed that he should feel so attracted to "female impersonator" Andrews while Karras, a closet gay, thinking his boss is that way too, confides in him what he really is. Garner is dumbfounded that this "bruising, macho, sonofabitching football player" is homosexual, which is precisely Edwards's comic point: that we tend to see people based on our clichéd images of their professions, that a professional athlete or other macho type can indeed be gay but no less manly for it. All these comic subversions of sexual stereotypes make *Victor/Victoria* one of the healthiest movies ever to come out of Hollywood.

Which is more than can be said of other gay-themed Hollywood movies of the late 70's through early 80's. From 1978 to 1982, there was a barrage of major studio films with gay themes, ranging in intent and quality from passable to inflammatory. These included the distortive drug-smuggling story *Midnight Express* (1978); *A Different Story* (1978), about a male-female gay couple who go straight; the timidly biographical *Nijinsky* (1980); the viciously anti-lesbian *Windows* (1980); the cardboard *Making Love* (1982); *Partners* (1982), an awful parody of *Cruising;* and the well-intended but dull *Personal Best* (1982), which at least had tender love scenes with Mariel Hemingway and Patrice Donnelly.

Except for *A Different Story* and *Personal Best,*

which at least strove to be authentic, these movies demonstrated that Hollywood producers and directors for the most part have a pathological distaste for homosexuals despite the fact that gays constitute a considerable percentage of the working talent on both sides of the camera. Discrimination against homosexual actors became even more rampant in 1985 and 1986 following the illness and death of Rock Hudson due to AIDS. Suddenly, many actresses were refusing to do love scenes with straight *or* gay actors because of the ignorant fear that AIDS was in the air and could be transmitted through a kiss or a hug. Though the understated, level-headed TV movie *An Early Frost* (1985) raised public awareness of the facts and realities of AIDS, to date there have been no theatrical films on the subject, though it is clearly a topic Hollywood will have to deal with, and on a continuing basis.

Surprisingly, the one gay film that took America by storm was the hilarious French cabaret comedy *La Cage aux Folles* (1978), directed by Edouardo Molinaro. It became *the* biggest gay box-office hit in American movie history, proving popular with gay and straight audiences alike. Like *The Boys in the Band,* it depicts gay stereotypes, especially the fluttering drag queen, but does so with lightning farcical speed, unpatronizing style and a non-stop procession of riotous gay jokes. You can feel uneasy over the stereotypes but you have to surrender yourself to belly laughs because it's so damned funny. Even so, the movie has a basic problem which is that we never understand why Ugo Tognazzi as the cabaret owner and Michel Serrault as his drag queen lover are attracted to each other; we never see any evidence of their mutual love. In fact, the most erotic scene is not between them, but between Tognazzi and ex-wife Claire Maurier when she tries to seduce him back to her bed.

Also from 1978 but not released in the U.S. until 1984 was the excellent Spanish film *El Diputado (The Deputy),* a drama of homosexual yearning set within the context of post-Franco political upheaval. It's a riveting case study of a Marxist homosexual congressman (Jose Sacristan) whose predilection for

Michael Ontkean and Kate Jackson in Making Love *(1982) come to grips with Ontkean's long-repressed homosexuality. The entire movie is as posed and artificial as this still.*

young hustlers—and one 16-year-old cupcake in particular (Jose L. Alonso)—leaves him wide open for blackmail by a right-wing group seeking to discredit the socialist left. *El Diputado* differs markedly from *Fox and His Friends* as a drama of class struggle because Eloy de la Eglesia's script, direction and editing create a dynamic saga of political and sexual tensions; we are excited because the story has passion and momentum. We end up rooting for Sacristan to beat the Francoists at their own conniving game because he is a decent, honorable, committed man, while knowing a happy ending is not fated. Moreover, his homosexuality is not seen as the result of marriage to a shrew—in fact, his chic, beautiful, sexy wife (Maria Louise San Jose) supports his need for male love because she loves and supports him as a person—but as the end product of an irresistible compulsion. It is this compulsion which is his political downfall and which makes *El Diputado* a profoundly moving tragedy.

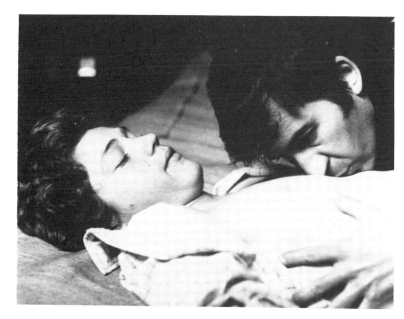

Despite the jeopardy to his career, Spanish socialist congressman Jose Sacristan in El Diputado *(*The Deputy, *1975) is smitten with lower-class teen hustler Jose Alonso. When sexy wife Maria Louise San Jose finds out, Alonso becomes her lover as well, as Sacristan looks on…then joins them for an intimate threesome. (Courtesy Award Films)*

A young Farrah Fawcett in bed with Myra Breckenridge *(Raquel Welch) (1970).*

As for lesbians, most American movies have treated them with contempt. *Windows* in 1980 became a cause célèbre because lesbian Elizabeth Ashley was a murderous rapist; Claudia Weill's *Girlfriends* (1978) viewed New York City lesbians with alarm; and Clint Eastwood's *Sudden Impact* (1983) had a bull dyke involved in a gang rape. The few realistic portrayals included the lesbian couple of Jane Alexander and Gena Rowlands waging a court battle for custody of Rowland's son in the TV movie *A Question of Love* (1978) and a sizzling drugstore scene in the notorious punks-on-the-run drama *The Warriors* (1979). In this scene, a gang of sexy teenage lesbians perform a steamy erotic dance to a thumping rock beat.

And then there are the porno movies, which feature lesbian scenes as a mechanical matter of course. One of the best of these is a movingly sensual one with Veronica Hart and Jessie St. James in *Indecent Exposure* (1982). It works because the direction and camerawork are sensitive, and because Hart and St. James are beautiful, charismatic women with libidinous chemistry.

Best of all is John Sayles's *Lianna* (1982), which is not only a masterpiece of lesbian love, but one of the greatest love stories ever filmed. It·has every element needed to raise it to the realm of uplifting art: a compelling story, humor, humanity, sensuality, visual poetry, unerringly human dialogue, and characters who become part of us.

Linda Griffiths, one of our most gifted actresses, is sensational in the title role as the alienated wife of an insensitive, adulterous film history teacher (Jon De-Vries) who finds romantic love with her psychology teacher, played with knowing compassion by Jane Hallaren. Their one bed scene is a knockout: a blue-filtered montage of sensual caresses and dissolves with breathless whispers on the soundtrack, culminating in the two women reveling in having found each other. There is also a wonderful 30-second montage as Griffiths grinningly ambles down a neighborhood street noticing women in a new way to the achingly romantic tune of "Nevertheless I'm in Love With You."

Lianna is filled with these moments, passionate but unsentimental, deepening our awareness of and insights into the nature and inherent tenderness of female love while filling us with bitter regret that these women can never publicly declare their love because it would ruin Hallaren's career; the sexual revolution did not extend that far. We are left with a poignantly ambiguous ending and the hope that Griffiths will someday find the woman of her dreams.

The best of homosexual cinema since 1970 is also like that, leaving us hopeful that furtive encounters in bars and toilets will no longer be necessary in years to come; that friendship, love and sex on their own

Title character Linda Griffiths (left) and lover Jane Hallaren relax with a cozy poolside tête-à-tête in John Sayles's masterpiece of lesbian love Lianna (1983). (Courtesy Landmark Theatres)

Jennifer West (on top) smooches with an unidentified player in A Little More Than Love (1980). (Courtesy William Margold)

Three concentration camp inmates in Ilsa, She Wolf of the SS *(1975) prepare to take revenge on a female Nazi. (Courtesy William Margold)*

merits will be cause for jubilation regardless of whether it is straight or gay. The message of the best of these movies is that we must evolve into a society in which homosexual men and women can find security and contentment with their sexual identities—mixed in with the inevitable hardships, heartaches and frustrations of any existence—if we are to consider ourselves truly democratic and peaceable. Most important of all, that when we learn to accept rather than stigmatize homosexuals for what they are, we will have learned, perhaps, to accept the bisexuality lurking in all of us.

That evolution and that acceptance, of course, are also up to all of us.

Chapter 3
INFIDELITY AND OTHER RELATIONSHIPS

"Any marriage is difficult to arrange and conduct successfully after the courtship is over. Group marriages are harder. You must be sure of the people you select. They are less than actual husbands and wives, even if you are intimate with them, but they are more than merely your best friends. It's kind of weird but wonderful when it works."—From the October, 1979, *Family Synergy* newsletter.

"The psychology of adultery has been falsified by conventional morals, which assume in monogamous countries that attraction to one person cannot coexist with a serious affection for another. Everybody knows that this is untrue."—From *Marriage and Morals* (1929) by Bertrand Russell.

We live in a society that outwardly espouses the monogamous heterosexual relationship: a man and a woman ceaselessly devoted to each other forever, never once thinking of other potential sex partners. The reality, of course, differs greatly from this impossible and perhaps unwanted ideal because most of us fantasize at one time or another about what it would be like to make love to someone other than our wives, husbands or lovers; to change our sexual diets and be free to experiment with as many people as possible without harmful emotional after effects. To have our liquor of libidinous intoxication with no danger of a climactic hangover. Most important of all, to have a quickie and not get caught at it.

Before the Hays Code was replaced by the rating system in the late 1960's, American movies could not accurately or imaginatively depict the reality/fantasy, pros and cons of adultery and promiscuity without twisting the outcome to suit a bogus moral code. Pre- or extra-marital sex could never be depicted as care-

free fun or as a complex chain of events unless the "guilty" parties were made to suffer the most severe punishments in the final reel: suicide, murder or madness.

Two actors who reflected this moral changing of the guard, becoming stars in the process, were Elliott Gould and Dyan Cannon in the trend-setting *Bob & Carol & Ted & Alice* (1969). Suddenly, the average-looking, diffident Gould and sensuous woman-next-door Cannon were the prototypes for the new screen image of open, hip sexuality without remorse, but with a price still to be paid as the Code gave a few last gasps.

No sooner had Cannon learned the joys of swinging without self-flagellation than she was punished for her promiscuity by being shot to death as a trollop in the first reel of the trashy *Doctors' Wives* (1970), and compelled to use sex as a weapon of jealous revenge against an errant husband in Otto Preminger's clichéd and dreary *Such Good Friends* (1970). In 1973, she

George Segal knows he has a good thing going with Glenda Jackson in A Touch of Class *(1973), keeping things light and friendly but not too involved.*

But the tables are turned when ex-wife Susan Anspach prefers rugged hippie Kris Kristofferson to him in Blume in Love *(1973)…*

…so, he starts his own easygoing post-marital affair with lovely Marsha Mason.

reverted to post-Code morality as James Coburn's lusty one-night stand in *The Last of Sheila*. For several years, Cannon became the free-spirited all-American slut, eventually transcending the image because she has always projected radiantly friendly sex appeal and screwball intelligence. In an about-face, she ended the 70's by experiencing the pain of being cheated on by country-singer husband Willie Nelson in the homey road movie *Honeysuckle Rose* (1980). Nelson, though, made it up to her by serenading his apology in the final reel.

Gould, on the other hand, made a brief career of playing hip, irreverent, free-wheeling professional men with a wandering eye in pictures like *M*A*S*H** and *Getting Straight* (both 1970). He embodied the late 60's, early 70's anarchist who taunts the mores of the social system from within. As if to atone for his unmoral brashness, he ended 1970 as a roaming doctor in the tepid *I Love My Wife,* infuriating wife Brenda Vaccaro with his compulsive duality as an idealistic M.D. by day and little-boy-on-the-loose in singles bars by night.

The quintessential movie adulterer of the 70's, though, was neither Gould nor Cannon but George Segal, who perfected the role in three movies that explored the ramifications of infidelity in the American middle-class. In *Loving* (1970), Segal is a hack ad illustrator striving desperately for success, placing a strain on his marriage to Eva Marie Saint. He will do anything to further his career, including lying and cheating, but it is a casual act of adultery at the posh home of a potential client that reveals him for the amoral heel he really is because his indiscretion is captured live on video camera for all of the party guests to see, to Saint's utter mortification.

Three years later, in 1973, Segal had two of his choicest roles in *A Touch of Class* and *Blume in Love,* further polishing his persona as a flip, earthy professional man who likes to dally on the side. In the former, he is a lawyer, apparently happily married, who is smitten with brittle dress designer Glenda Jackson. Their Yankee-Britannia chemistry is immediate, propelling them into a romantic if misadventurous week in Spain and a prolonged series of trysts in Soho, London, in the *Back Street* tradition.

Beneath the glib laughs and carnal camaraderie of these goings on is the sober realization that the affair cannot last because the relationship is lopsided. Jackson yearns for the permanence of commitment while Segal hypocritically wants the best of both worlds: marital respectability (we never do learn what kind of woman his wife is) and a waiting mistress. In the end, you wonder if any relationship based on one-way give-and-take is worth the emotional drain. Yet, in real life, single women fall for married men all the time—and vice-versa—and with just as little hope of commitment.

In *Blume in Love,* Segal is caught in the act with his secretary by wife Susan Anspach, who immediately divorces him. He then doggedly tries to win her back because her love is worth more to him than an impulsive moment of illicit passion. Gone is the cocky lawyer of *A Touch of Class* and in his place is a more reflective, sensitized man. Yet, for all its striving to be comically honest, Paul Mazursky's script never answers the questions of why Anspach is so quick to devalue her marriage to Segal by getting rid of him after one indiscretion, or why, if she is so zealous about fidelity, she wastes no time moving in with rugged hippie Kris Kristofferson, a man less liable to remain one-on-one than Segal. You wonder how solid their marriage was to start with.

Other movies of the early to late 70's busied themselves depicting the consequences of unlicensed relationships, ranging from the comic to the bizarre. In Billy Wilder's easygoing, under-rated *Avanti* (1972), Jack Lemmon and Juliet Mills take up where their respective parents left off; *The Heartbreak Kid* (1972) had fickle Charles Grodin married to whining Jewish American Princess Jeannie Berlin while lusting after golden-haired WASP Cybil Shepherd; the satiric *Network* (1976) injected a gratuitous affair between William Holden and Faye Dunaway which nevertheless reaches a comic high point when Holden dines and beds Dunaway as she incessantly chatters about TV deals and ratings; Burt Reynolds, Jill Clayburgh and Kris Kristofferson enjoyed an easygoing but sexless ménage-à-trois in the scattershot fad satire *Semi-Tough* (1976); hawkish Jane Fonda made love to handicapped Vietnam vet Jon Voight in *Coming Home* (1978) while hubby Bruce Dern was off fighting the Viet Cong; and a computer programmed by scientist Fritz Weaver in *Demon Seed* (1977) took on a megalomaniac life of its own by forcibly impregnating Weaver's wife Julie Christie to spawn its evil progeny.

An oasis of comic sanity in the midst all these variations on a theme was Woody Allen's superbly inventive *Play it Again, Sam* (1972, directed by Herbert Ross), one of those rare movies that leaves you feeling refreshed and whole. The issue here is not so much the rightness or wrongness of an affair, though that is dealt with too, but rather learning to overcome one's deepest fears of acting like a total jerk in pursuit of a relationship. Allen falls in love with his best friend's wife—his first teaming with Diane Keaton—as she helps him attain sexual self-confidence after his divorce.

When the inevitable night of love happens, Allen feels no remorse, only a surge of pride over his newly found virility. "I'm a man and you're a woman," he

In I Love My Wife *(1970) happily (?) married Elliott Gould has a blissful affair with Joanna Cameron.*

Jack Lemmon and Juliet Mills savor the delicious aftermath of a night of illicit love in Avanti *(1972), though Lemmon is clearly having second thoughts.*

William Holden in Network *(1976) is serious about Faye Dunaway, telling her he wants more than sex and constant prattle about TV shows.*

matter-of-factly states, "and that's what those kind of people do."

Topping it all off, when Allen confesses his adultery to Keaton's husband, Tony Roberts, in a direct lift from the finale of *Casablanca,* Roberts takes it in sympathetic stride, knowing that Keaton was only a safety valve for Allen's pent-up neuroses. Now that Allen feels more confident of his manliness and self-worth, he can stride with the ghost of Bogart (Jerry Lacy), his idol and literally spiritual mentor, into the airport fog.

One of the cause célèbres of screen sex of the early 70's was Bernardo Bertolucci's X-rated *Last Tango in Paris* (1973), about a far less affectionate affair, what Erica Jong would later call the "zipless fuck": two strangers meeting briefly, enjoying a moment of pure passion, then parting as strangers. Totally anonymous sex, no strings, no bitter aftertaste. This is what Marlon Brando aims for with Maria Schneider and one of the reasons film critic Pauline Kael compared the film to Stravinsky's *Rite of Spring:* for its cinematic and emotional impact in terms of shockingly sexual realism.

For all the critical hype, *Last Tango in Paris* is actually a dull affair—and soft-core at that—coming to life only when Brando is on screen. Though it's initially titillating to watch a super-star engage in kinky sex acts with a young woman (remember the infamous butter scene?), there is nothing you really bring away from this film except relief that it's over. It will probably be remembered more for the sensation it caused as the first X film with a major star than for any lasting impact on the cinema.

Even more sensational were two other controversial foreign imports: Lina Wertmuller's *Swept Away by an Unusual Destiny in the Blue Sea of August* (1974), and Nagisa Oshima's ravishingly pornographic *In the Realm of the Senses* (1976). In the former, adultery becomes a riveting confrontation between members of opposite social classes, while in both films sex for its own sake becomes a maelstrom of obsessive carnal possession.

In *Swept Away,* when an angry, foul-mouthed seaman (Giancarlo Giannini) is cast away with a chattering upper-class magpie (Mariangelo Melato), he

Julie Christie in Demon Seed *(1977) is wired up by mad scientist hubby Fritz Weaver to be impregnated by a computer.*

Meanwhile, Diane Keaton in Play it Again Sam *(1972) frets about her night of love with Woody Allen.*

Adultery could be fatally all-consuming as in The Realm of the Senses *(1976), in which former geisha Eiko Matsuda and brothel keeper Tatsuya Fuji become sexually inseparable...*

uses pure animal sex and verbal humiliation to bring her down to his earthier class level, converting her from the smug respectability of a materialistic marriage to the stormy wantonness of submissive lust. The movie is a literal depiction of poet Sylvia Plath's admonition that "Every woman loves a fascist," angering a lot of feminists in the process.

Even more erotically disturbing is the Oshima film, based on a true story, the intrigue of which is the psychopathology that would motivate a woman to the seemingly depraved act of severing her lover's penis. The motivation here is obsessive lust: a geisha turned brothel maid is swept into an affair with her employer's smart-ass stud husband and they become so self-absorbed sexually that they cannot bear *not* to make love constantly; acts that are shown in graphic, pseudo-artful detail. When he dies during orgasm, she mutilates him in a final act of crazed devotion.

For all the heated debate engendered by *In the Realm of the Senses* over its artistic and erotic merits, the truth is that it owes its notoriety more to the hype surrounding it (the result of originally being banned by U.S. Customs, making it a must-see hot item) than to its actual value as erotic entertainment, insightful or otherwise. There is plenty of straightforward hardcore sex in this movie but none of it is erotically compelling. The problem is that Oshima was more concerned with making an artful sex film than with making an involving sex film. He sets up his premise in the first reel and plunges us headlong into an endless series of progressively repulsive sex acts—a hardboiled egg shoved into a vagina, then devoured by the stud, for example—without taking the time to explore the characters or the sexual psychology behind their obsessiveness. The result is a pretentious so-called art film that is boring and disgusting and which leaves a foul aftertaste, especially with its disturbing mutilation finale.

Oshima returned to this theme of adulterous lust with less commercial success in *Empire of Passion* (1978), an arty, symbol-heavy, boring remake of *The Postman Always Rings Twice* set in feudal Japan. Here, he was more concerned with pseudo-profound shock effects than with realistic drama, undercutting his impact and leaving a foul taste. There was also a bitter aftertaste to Bob Rafelson's American remake of

...leading to orgasm by strangulation, followed by Matsuda castrating Fuji as an ultimate form of sexual devotion. (Courtesy Landmark Theatres)

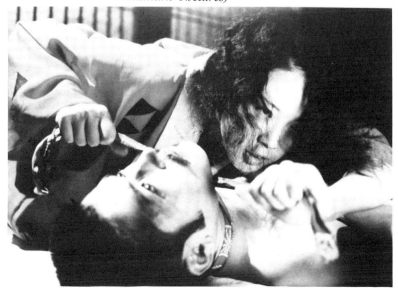

In Cousin, Cousine *(1975), adulterous cousins Victor Lanoux and Marie-Christine Barrault playfully draw patterns on each other while bathing.*

Postman (1981) with Jack Nicholson and Jessica Lange, but for a different reason. What Hollywood couldn't show in 1946 in this tale of two lovers conniving to kill the woman's husband for insurance money, Rafelson could, and that was the problem. Rutting softcore sex with no erotic undertones or depth of character is no substitute for solid, witty, well-acted storytelling. Tay Garnett's classic original was impeded by the censors, but there is so much implicit erotic tension between John Garfield and Lana Turner you hardly notice. After 35 years, less turned out to be a hell of a lot more.

Not all treatments of adultery were fraught with melodrama and violence. The delightful French comedy *Cousin, Cousine* (1975) told the piquant tale of two cousins by marriage (Marie-Christine Barrault and

Victor Lanoux) who go beyond easygoing friendship to kindred romantic love, finding a lot more in common with each other than with their respective spouses. Her husband is a philandering louse; his wife no longer sparks him. They happily respond to each other's innately whimsical nature, ending up as you hope they will and damn the relatives.

Adultery could also have long-term commitment, as in Robert Mulligan's neglected gem *Same Time, Next Year* (1978), in which Alan Alda and Ellen Burstyn meet for a yearly weekend tryst from the early 50's to the late 70's. Because the movie does cover a 26-year span, we can see the characters evolving, changing with the times and each other. For a rare change, we are shown that adultery can involve far more than sex; it can lead to lasting, intimate friendship.

There are also alternatives to conventional adultery: Open or group marriage, lifestyles that go beyond so-called cheating into the more rarified realms of loving secondary relationships and dual or multiple spouses; interactive sharing that negates the need for jealousy precisely because those involved recognize that no one person can satisfy all of an individual's needs. Several real-life organizations promote these lifestyles, one of the most notable being the Los Angeles-based Family Synergy, which holds monthly seminars.

Few movies, though (especially American ones), have dared to deal with these lifestyles. The few examples that come to mind include the free-spirited ménage-à-trois of Michael Ontkean, Margot Kidder and Ray Sharkey in *Willie and Phil* (1980); Glenn Close in *The Big Chill* (1983) coaxing husband Kevin Kline into impregnating close family friend Mary Kay Place, a rare example of sexual sharing in American cinema; Gerard Depardieu seeking lovers for his sexually dormant wife (Carol Laure) in the divinely offbeat French comedy *Get Out Your Handkerchiefs* (1978); and the most famous open marriage exponent of the 70's and 80's, Sylvia Kristel in the *Emmanuelle* series from France, begun in 1974 by former commercials director Just Jaeckin (pronounced Jahkeen).

Jack Nicholson and Jessica Lange in The Postman Always Rings Twice *(1981) were also caught up in a heat wave of lust, consummating their desire before plotting to murder Lange's husband for money.*

Michael Ontkean (left), Margot Kidder and Ray Sharkey in Willie and Phil *(1980): They look as though they've just had a dandy sexual threesome or are about to. Either way, theirs is a consummate three-way partnership.*

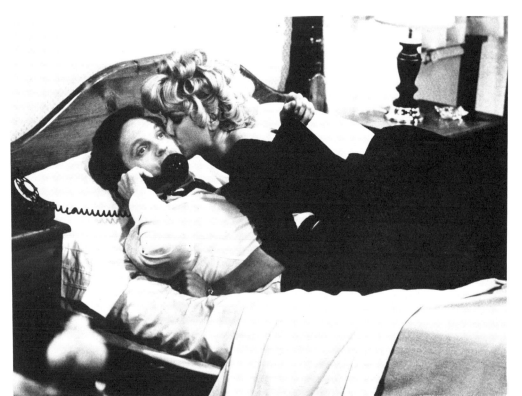

In Same Time, Next Year *(1978) Alan Alda is in the midst of his yearly rendezvous with smoochy Ellen Burstyn when he is startled by a call from home.*

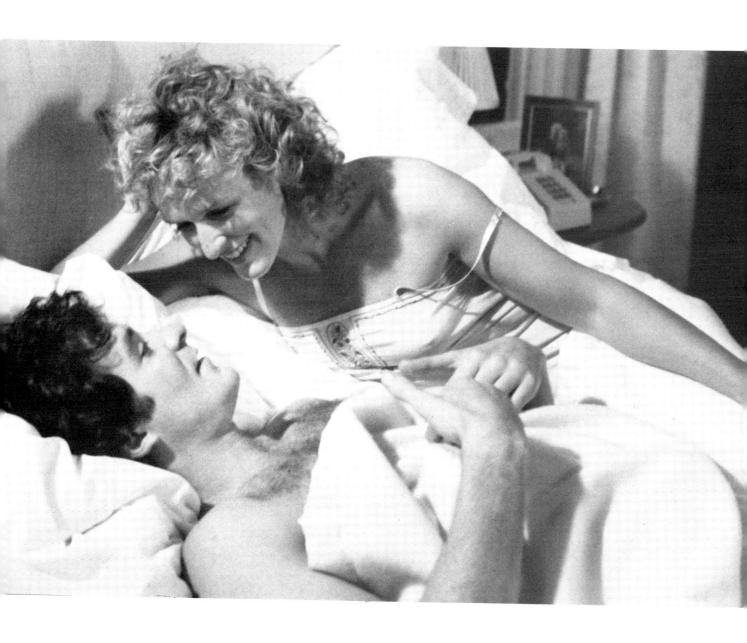

*Glenn Close talks husband Kevin Kline into
sharing himself with an unwed close friend
who wants a child, in* The Big Chill *(1983).*

Gerard Depardieu (left) in Get Out Your Handkerchiefs *(1978) hoped that Patrick Dewaere could spark some life into his somnolent wife, Carol Laure. She just kept on knitting until she found…*

…Riton, a precociously sensitive teenager who awakened her long dormant feelings of love and tenderness. By film's end, they have had a child, leaving Depardieu and Dewaere out in the cold. (Courtesy Landmark Theatres)

The series centers on a free-swinging Bangkok diplomat who encourages his child bride Kristel to expand her sexual horizons by experimenting with various lovers, both male and female, while he enjoys his own sexual license. Kristel's teacher and guide is a distinguished-looking gent (Alain Cuny) who chatters endlessly about breaking down old moral codes and releasing all inhibitions, but in the end all he really does is subject Kristel to public anal sex, rape and other brutalities, while he stands nearby watching impassively. For a man given to sexual freedom, Cuny is curiously devoid of humor, never once smiling or displaying any feelings.

What made *Emmanuelle* a commercial success was less its meager dramatic merits—though the film is pictorially lush—than the fact that the time was right and Kristel had an undeniable screen presence, conveying erotic curiosity beneath her innocent exterior.

Emmanuelle II: The Joys of a Woman *(1975). Sylvia Kristel has husband-approved extramarital fling with a woman (Catherine Rivet).*

Emmanuelle II: The Joys of a Woman. *The cocktail hour in old Bangkok.*

Emmanuelle II: The Joys of a Woman *(1975)*.

Sonia Braga in Dona Flor and Her Two Husbands *(1981) literally had the best of two worlds: making passionate love to errant husband Jose Wilker in life…*
…and to his naked corporeal spirit in death while enduring respectfully conventional sex with staid husband number two, Mauro Mendoca. (Courtesy Landmark Theatres)

Emmanuelle II: The Joys of a Woman (1975) was also a success and it seemed that the series had concluded with *Goodbye Emmanuelle* in 1978, but 1985 brought the announcement of an *Emmanuelle IV,* as if to find out if a mature Kristel in the old softcore formula still works commercially. In the long run, the *Emmanuelle* series is more of an excuse for endless bouts of beautifully photographed but boring softcore sex than it is a serious platform for dramatizing an alternate lifestyle.

A sexier film by far than *Emmanuelle,* ending with group marriage of a wacky sort, was the zesty Brazilian comedy *Dona Flor and Her Two Husbands* (1977), in which lustful Sonia Braga ends up with the best of two worlds: her respectable, upright, dull second husband and her fiery, womanizing, very dead first husband, whose naked and amazingly corporeal spirit sates the passions left unquenched by hubby number two. The movie's final shot implies that every woman really wants two men in one: a good citizen/provider and a red-hot lover.

Despite the few attempts to show that adultery didn't have to be a crime, conventional infidelity continued to be big boxoffice in the late 70's and early 80's, though with a few twists. Our premier adulterer, self-imagined cuckold and roaming daydreamer during that time was undeniably that elfin charmer, Dudley Moore. He hit it big in *10* (1979) as a randy songwriter who forsakes his mature, intelligent girlfriend, Julie Andrews, to lust after newly married Bo Derek, only to discover that beneath all that surface beauty is a bubble-headed exponent of free love. Moreover, his sexual candy bar has seduced *him,* giving him back his own spoonful of infidelity, making him a hypocrite. His fantasy shattered and his senses restored, Moore heads back to the less physically gorgeous but more emotionally satisfying Andrews, who at least is interested in him as a person beyond momentary sexual gratification. Blake Edwards's point is well-taken: that a relationship with substance is worth far more than one fantasy fling or scores of them.

Moore's second romantic comedy for Blake Edwards was again a suitable vehicle for his considerable comic charm. In *Micki and Maude* (1984), he is bigamously married to Ann Reinking and Amy Irving, getting them both pregnant; he is dying to raise a family. Though the two wives eventually discover what is going on, vowing to cast him out of their lives, they cannot hate him for long because they love him for the good-hearted soul he really is. Again Edwards scores a provocative comic point: that bigamy isn't necessarily a heinous emotional crime, that it can be a civilized and nurturing three-way affair if the people involved are right for each other as they are here. One wonders, though, with the audience pulling for Moore to have it

In 10 *(1979), Dudley Moore fantasized making love to perfect-looking specimen Bo Derek, only to discover when* she *seduced* him *that she had more body than brains.*

In Micki and Maude *(1984), he went even further by bigamously impregnating Amy Irving…*

…and *first wife Ann Reinking. But Moore was such a charming, cuddly fellow you really couldn't help wanting him to get away with both marriages…which he does.*

Handsome jock Mark Soper in The World According to Garp *(1982) lusts after teacher Mary Beth Hurt, who warns him that she is married. They start an affair anyway, leading to tragedy for both of them.*

This moment of adulterous angst is brought to you by Ann-Margret and Gene Hackman in the utterly mundane Twice in a Lifetime *(1985).*

both ways, why Edwards didn't go all the way with a more expansive and richer comic statement about the merits of group marriage vs. monogamy instead of two reels of contrived, predictable farce at the end. The movie climaxes with a final shot implying a bigamous group marriage, but it's more of an effect than the end result of a series of inventive comic scenes building to that shot.

While Edwards and Moore were making us laugh about infidelity and group marriage by way of making us think about them, other movies were hewing more closely to modern, everyday adultery, including *Urban Cowboy* (1980), *Terms of Endearment* (1983) and *Twice in a Lifetime* (1985). What the first two have in common is Debra Winger, cheating on her husband in both movies to get even with him.

In *Urban Cowboy* (the movie that made her a star), she marries handsome hick John Travolta after the briefest of courtships, then finds that when she proves herself his equal on a mechanical bull at Gilley's Bar and Grill, his macho pride is wounded; in fact, he has one hell of a masculinity problem. More than that. When they come home after his night riding on the bull, Travolta complains, "My balls are killing me." To which Winger worriedly replies, "Does that mean we won't be able to do it?" This hilarious exchange is revealing because it tells us that Travolta is more concerned with maintaining a phony image of macho bravado than with maintaining a happy marriage, which is certainly more important. He thinks he wants a more passively domestic woman who won't try to be his equal, so he has an affair with one, while she thinks she will be happier with macho outlaw Scott Glenn. They are both wrong and the film ends with them reuniting after realizing that their mutual false pride is no substitute for a secure union based on their real love for each other.

Winger's adultery in *Terms of Endearment* is a slightly different sort because it is based on mutual loneliness. She has a series of trysts with diffident, sex-starved bank officer John Lithgow (his wife is frigid), partly because she is charmed by his warm genuineness, partly to get even with her sneak of a husband. The affair is short-lived (the best scenes were deleted for time), but a good one, with no lingering regrets. Life must go on. What is even more important here socially is mass audience acceptance of this affair because sympathy for Winger signals a commonplace public attitude (remember, this movie was a huge commercial hit) toward extra-marital sex based on circumstance and identification with that circumstance.

Less sympathetic is the adulterous affair of Gene Hackman and Ann-Margaret in the vastly overrated

Out of Africa *(1985): Stifled by her loveless marriage to a nobleman, Meryl Streep finds passion in the arms of Robert Redford.*

Mrs. Soffel *(1984): Prisoner Mel Gibson startles pious warden's wife Diane Keaton (Mrs. Soffel) with a passionate kiss in hope of seducing her into helping him escape.*

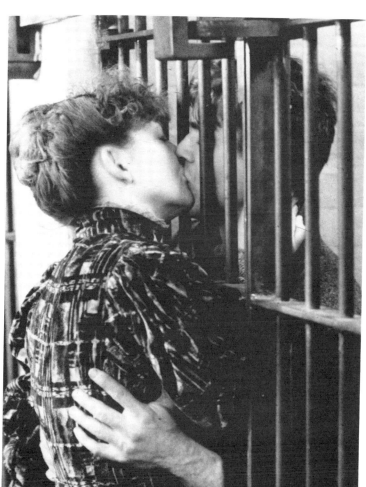

Hannah and her Sisters *(1986): In Woody Allen's ode to mixed-up sexual relationships, Michael Caine is happily beside himself with love for Barbara Hershey, his wife's sister, while she has mixed feelings for him.*

Twice in a Lifetime. What is supposed to make this movie special is that instead of leaving his dull, mousy wife for a much younger woman, steelworker Hackman starts an affair with mid-forties barmaid Margaret on his fiftieth birthday. Though director Bud Yorkin tried to make this an insightful and compelling drama about modern adultery and divorce, it is nothing more than an average, clichéd and rambling textbook movie on those themes, with Hackman virtually walking through his role giving the right expressions. We never get a handle on his character or why his marriage to Ellen Burstyn has fallen apart, so we can never give a damn that he is hurting his family with his affair. All you can think about this empty, boring movie is that you've seen it before…and

before…and before.

If there is any one message about extramarital sex conveyed by movies of the 70's and 80's, it is that without a hypocritical movie code, filmmakers are freer to tell realistic human stories with several levels of depth and substance, with comedy and tears. They can cut through the games people play with eros to the fantasies and desires that really motivate and plague us, and to the often cold realities that ensue when those fantasies become real. Marriage isn't the only type of sexual partnership, but in all its forms it can be the most satisfying way of life if the partners are right for and tolerant and accepting of each other's needs and foibles. At their best, movies can influence us toward more rational behavior in situations where hasty decisions can lead to years of painful regret and loneliness.

Chapter 4
PROSTITUTES

"You make a man think that he's accepted. It's all just a big game to you. You prey upon the sexual fantasies of others. That's your stock in trade, a man's weaknesses, and I was never really fully aware of mine until *you* brought them out."—Charles Cioffi in *Klute*.

"What's *your* bag, Klute? What do *you* like? You a talker, a button freak? Love to have your chest walked on with high-heeled shoes? Maybe you like to have us watch you tinkle. Or do you get it off wearing women's clothes? Goddamn hypocrite squares!"—Jane Fonda in *Klute*.

Prostitutes, Hookers. Whores. Ladies of the evening. Fallen women. Streetwalkers. Working girls. Courtesans. By whatever name they're called, they provide honest, uninhibited, uninvolved sexual relief for a price, catering to an infinite variety of whims, fantasies and kinks. And Hollywood has been having a love affair with them for decades, precisely because their brazen antics are a turn-on and lure moviegoers—especially men—like an erotic magnet.

When the movie code was in force, you couldn't call a whore a whore except in rare non-Production Code movies like *Never on Sunday* or *Elmer Gantry* (both 1960). Actresses could only imply the trade through context, clothes, make-up and a certain air of lively vulgarity or jaded experience. Prostitutes were either heart-of-gold or hard-as-nails types. Nor were they characters with very much depth or feeling. They were mainly stereotypes for background color, to act as a scapegoat for a gag, or to prove a contrived moral point that whoring can only lead to shame, degrada-

tion, alcoholism and/or suicide, and a social status as outcast with no hope of marrying into a "respectable" bourgeois family. Never mind that the women who turn tricks in real life are often intelligent, thoughtful, considerate people with ambitions and goals beyond life in the street or in the whorehouse. The very fact that they serve as a vessel for lust has always been used to make them seem less than human.

Then too, there is the proverbial madonna/whore complex whereby a woman is seen as helpmate or skilled sexual partner, never both. With this view, a woman is either a lady or a tramp, with aggressive sexual behavior tagging her as the latter. This sluttish image is largely why so many men turn to prostitutes: hookers give them what they can't get at home or for which they are afraid to ask, especially anal sex, oral sex and domination, in that order. "Nice" women—meaning their wives—don't do those things.

Since 1970, of course, prostitutes have been portrayed on screen with much greater complexity, vari-

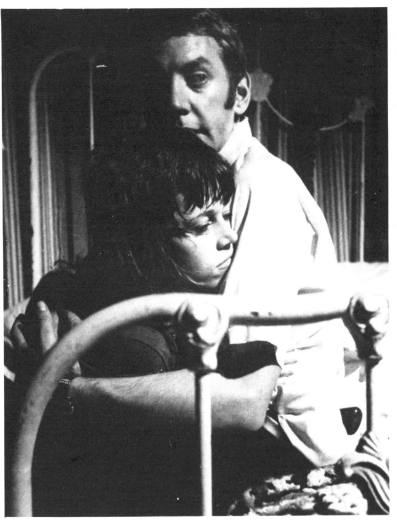

High-class call girl Jane Fonda finds unexpected comfort with stoic detective Donald Sutherland when her life is threatened in Klute *(1971).*

ety and sympathy: straight, gay and bisexual men and women; psychopaths; nymphomaniacs; good old girls; schizophrenics; teenagers; and career-minded adults trying to pay the bills while pursuing a longer-term professional goal such as acting. Stereotypes do persist, but prostitutes have increasingly been depicted as real people with real problems, hangups, senses of humor, imaginations, and a need for romantic, domes-

tic love like anyone else. And yet, in all these views of the world of play-for-pay, there has seldom been a suggestion that prostitution be legalized, let alone a full-scale depiction of the social and other consequences if it were. There is grist for a superb comedy in that premise and no one has tapped it. But then, its quality of illicit pleasure has always been prostitution's greatest allure, and a box-office gold mine.

One of the commonest images of the hooker is as an instrument for male rites of passage. Who better to make a boy a man than the neighborhood strumpet or local bordello queen? Raunchy career sailor Jack Nicholson didn't hesitate to take court-martialed sailor Randy Quaid to a whorehouse for his initiation in *The Last Detail* (1973), though Quaid jumped the gun when Carol Kane barely touched him; Matt Lattanzi joined his goofball buddies on a rowdy outing to an L.A. house in *My Tutor* (1983), only to have one of the buddies end up being scared out of what little wits he had by a whip-wielding dominatrix; a team of victorious good old boy football players were treated to a Sunday picnic-like outing to the Chicken Ranch by governor Robert Mandan in *The Best Little Whorehouse in Texas* (1982), culminating in a rousing yee-haw square dance; a gang of naive, anxiously horny teens were lined up for "venereal" inspection by Cherry Forever (Susan Clark) in *Porky's* (1981); and teenage shutterbug Jonathan Cryer was extremely shy with a lovely and gentle hooker (Maureen Ann Schatzberg) in *No Small Affair* (1984). Clearly, the prostitute is as much a part of our native American folkloric rituals as the Fourth of July.

There is also the view from the streets, where prostitutes are known as "working girls" and are usually dependent on overdressed, abusive pimps for their livelihood and lifestyle. Three contrasting movies offer differing perspectives on women looking for fast pickups and quick, easy money. In the excellent TV movie *Hustling* (1975), Lee Remick is an investigative journalist who has her eyes opened to the sordid world of tricks and pimps by hooker Jill Clayburgh. She gives Remick a crash course on what it's like to walk those mean urban streets, privy to and satisfying the often kinky urges of affluent middle- and upper-middle-class gents whose wives are apparently a prudish and frigid lot. Because it was made for the small screen, *Hustling* is not sexually explicit, yet that

Macho sailor James Caan takes a stroll along a sleazy boulevard with prostitute girlfriend Marsha Mason in Cinderella Liberty *(1973).*

*Amply endowed madam
Dolly Parton gives some
gaping local yokels a good
look-see…*

...at her singing, dancing whores at The Best Little Whorehouse in Texas *(1982).*

But that's nothing compared to the rousing victory dance the local football team is treated to before they get down to business. *Something dirty* is going on.

is all to the good because Fay Kanin's superb script forces the viewer to pay serious attention to what this seamy world is all about, to think about the psychological and moral side effects of catering to men's needs and being dependent on a pimp for your own.

Conversely, the underrated *Vice Squad* (1982), with its *Hill Street Blues*-like look and feel, goes wide open with its view of Los Angeles as an inferno of corruption, a modern-day Sodom and Gomorrah begging to be blown off the map. *Vice Squad* titillates as it reveals a hellish world of victims and victimizers: the constant arrests and harassment of streetwalkers by cops whose daily grind has drained them of compassion; the masochistically naive teenage girls who let themselves be beaten to death by psychotic pimps in the belief that bruises and blood are a proof of love; the dependence on pimps to provide bail-out money and a decent lifestyle away from work, albeit as part of a stable of "bitches"; and the constant pressure to perform sex acts according to the customer's needs. As one hooker puts it: "No one wants straight sex anymore!"

In 1980's Los Angeles, this is absolutely true. In a December 8, 1985, *Los Angeles Times* article titled "Life in the Street: New Wave of Prostitution with More Violence Is Overwhelming L.A. Authorities," writer Miles Corwin both catalogues the disgustingly strange scenarios L.A. hookers are often compelled to enact for money, and details the increasing real-life violence against them by their clients. The latter includes sadistic beatings, harrowing tortures and serial murders of prostitutes by psychopathic customers, especially by one black murderer known as the Southside Serial Killer who has been terrorizing Los Angeles for three years. This article makes it clear that for all its seedy, tense, hammering realism, *Vice Squad* doesn't go nearly far enough in depicting the dangers of streetwalking in the City of Angels; though only a few years old, already it's a movie behind the sordid reality of the times.

And yet, compare the depressingly realistic tone of *Vice Squad* with its comic counterpart in *Night Shift* (1982), a delightfully offbeat movie directed by Ron

The real business of whoring: Money exchanged for services rendered. Season Hubley as seasoned pro Princess in Vice Squad *(1981).*

Henry Winkler surrounded by the belles of the night he and Michael Keaton are pimping out of the New York City morgue in Night Shift *(1982). That's adorable Shelley Long at Winkler's immediate left.*

Howard. The plot revolves around nebbishy Henry Winkler (his best film role to date) and maniacally flaky Michael Keaton concocting a scheme to run a prostitution ring out of the New York City morgue, ensuring that working girls like Shelley Long get a steady stream of satisfied clients and 90 percent of the take, as opposed to a mere 10 percent from their vicious pimps. Whereas *Vice Squad* for all its dead-on vividness leaves you with a dirty feeling and a contempt for humanity, *Night Shift* leaves you feeling refreshed because it is sharp, witty and good-natured. You sympathize with these women because they're only trying to make a living at what they do best, and

For all the hookers he deals with in Night Shift *(1982), Henry Winkler is sexually aroused only by Shelley Long.*

Mathieu Carriere (left) and Gudrun Land-grebe share a post-coital cigarette in A Woman in Flames *(1982) prior to her learning that they also share the same profession.*

you root for the odd couple of Winkler and Keaton because they *are* ensuring efficient, clean, quality service. *Vice Squad* is more brutally realistic but *Night Shift* has a far more humane view of prostitution. Moreover, when Winkler falls for Long (who gives a sweet and sexy performance), she becomes his soul-mate and sex partner, the woman who helps him get his bearings.

A step up from the common street hooker is the call girl, meeting men in their apartments or hotel rooms via phone contacts or referrals. A series of exploitation films have been devoted to the erotic escapades of the world's most famous call girl, Xaviera Hollander, but only Martine Beswicke did her justice in the otherwise tacky *The Happy Hooker Goes Holly-wood* (1980), conveying the sultry maturity and kinky charm of the real Hollander.

The call girl who left the most indelible impres-sion was Jane Fonda's Bree Daniels in *Klute* (1971), winning Fonda a well-deserved Oscar for her wide-ranging portrayal of a hooker seeing a psychiatrist for her loss of feeling while aspiring to be an actress, a trade where feeling is crucial. Daniels's problem is the numbness that comes from experiencing the lower depths of human nature in ten thousand strange bedrooms. When she meets detective John Klute (Donald Sutherland)—a normal, decent, quiet man—she discovers to her amazement that not everyone with a penis is out to leech on her, to use her body and run. When Klute makes love to her, accepting her as and for what she is, the resulting surge of long dormant emotions both excites and scares Daniels, setting in motion a powerful inner conflict between going with the flow and walling herself up again.

Prostitution as a dead-end is also the theme of Robert Van Ackeren's *A Woman in Flames* (1983, q.v. also chapter on Kinky Sex), but it's hard to care in this case because this tale of two whores—a bisexual gigolo (Mathieu Carriere) and a bar girl turned domi-natrix (Gudrun Landgrebe)—is so elliptical in style that we never get to know these characters as people. Ackeren relies on meaningful looks and a dour tone at the expense of exposition, characterization and a sense of humor. That many blanks make *A Woman in Flames* a cold, empty, hostile exercise in kinky sex cum social commentary rather than the scathing, cathartic morality play on passionless sex most critics make it out to be. One can understand its popularity in West Germany because it has sprinklings of straight sex, gay sex, bi-sex and kinky sex, but those commer-cial elements alone don't add up to anything. Too much else is missing, including a heart.

Another kinky cause célèbre, *Crimes of Passion* (1984), also has a lot missing: a coherent plot, credible characters and disciplined direction by Ken Russell.

Clean-cut married man John Laughlin finds himself caught up in a maelstrom of sexual passion with street hooker Kathleen Turner in Crimes of Passion *(1984).*

It's about a schizo (Kathleen Turner) who is a dress designer by day, a sultry hooker by night named China Blue who has a lavish array of costumes ranging from smart-looking B&D (bondage and discipline) attire to a nun's outfit! There's a fair amount of softcore action here, but the most graphic scenes were eliminated to bring the film down from an X to an R.

Though the two sequences dropped add nothing to the movie except dubious prurient value, Russell complained that his integrity was being violated. These two sequences were restored for home video, resulting in blockbuster cassette sales for New World Video. They comprise: 1) a 2½-minute sequence showing Turner and John Laughlin enacting the Kama Sutra in silhouette while Tony Perkins feverishly watches through a peephole; and 2) a 2-minute sequence in which Turner ties a masochistic cop to a bed for some rough-and-tumble sadism, drawing

blood with spurs. The intensity of this latter sequence derives from rapid-fire editing in the best tradition of manipulative montage. This sequence also explains why it is that Turner's China Blue is shaken to tears in the following scene. But, for all their bogus intensity, these sequences do not make the movie any more involving or less unattractive.

Crimes of Passion is supposed to be an examination of prostitution as the road to schizoid misery, but it's nothing more than empty, sleazy pretense. It hammers us with pseudo-philosophical banter, never explains why psychotic pseudo-preacher Tony Perkins—virtually reprising Norman Bates from *Psycho*—fastens on her as his victim for salvation, and is just one long, silly exercise in banal titillation. It's a remake of *Rain* by way of *Belle de Jour* minus a brain. The best line is when Perkins tells Turner: "You wear your anguish like a breakaway chastity belt." The worst

Succulent virgin Brooke Shields is offered to the highest bidder in Pretty Baby *(1978).*

thing about all of this is that because of the home video market, even though *Crimes of Passion* was a theatrical flop, it is a private-use success.

In this parade of prosties, there is also the teen hooker, the strutting jailbait acting as high-priced lure for pedophiles. Young flesh for sale has always held special appeal for men, especially those in middle age. It supposedly allows them to vicariously make love to their daughters, but more important, teen hookers are pretty and ostensibly unmarked by time or experience.

The two most controversial teen prostitutes since 1970 have been Brooke Shields in Louis Malle's New Orleans period piece *Pretty Baby* (1978), and Jodie Foster in Martin Scorsese's *Taxi Driver* (1976). Both films attempt to comment on the sexual corruption of the young. Shields was talked about because here was the country's foremost teen model/actress flaunting her sex appeal in a blatantly erotic setting. Though the

movie was well-intended, it seemed more of an excuse for a well-mounted pedophiliac dream than a serious drama about the emotional consequences of raising a girl in a brothel.

Taxi Driver, on the other hand, engendered heated debate over its graphically bloody violence in the final reel, and over Foster's precociously dynamic portrayal of a street-wise teen whore runaway. The importance of the film to this discussion is that it dives headlong into the madonna/whore complex. Robert DeNiro's psychopathic title character is obsessed with Foster because, like Don Quixote, he sees her as a teenage Dulcinea, not as the hard-bitten hooker she really is. He is determined to lead her from the prone position to a pedestal, butting in where he isn't wanted, certainly not by Foster.

Taxi Driver is a jazzier film cinematically than *Pretty Baby*—Bernard Herrmann's pulsing final score is one of its major assets—but while it does make you

Jodie Foster caused a sensation playing a streetwise teen hooker in Taxi Driver *(1976).*

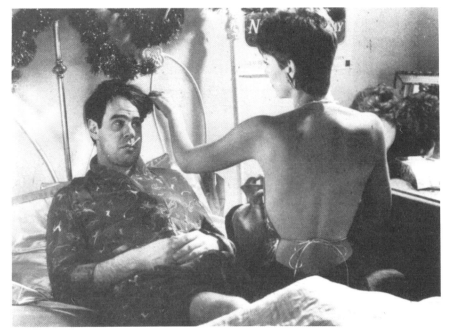

Parental guidance got a switch in The World According to Garp *(1982) when Glenn Close (right) approached hooker Swoosie Kurtz on behalf of her writer son Robin Williams, embarrassing the hell out of him. Kurtz eventually becomes a friend of the family.*

Sassy streetwalker Jamie Lee Curtis in Trading Places *(1983) helps Dan Aykroyd recover from the flu so he can get even with the s.o.b.s who set him up for a fall.*

Clergyman Michael Palin saves a fallen woman by falling with her in The Missionary *(1982).*

wonder about all the teenagers taking to the streets as prostitutes, the subtheme is lost in the final shootout and the film's overall view of New York City as a moral wasteland, pockmarked with vice and worthless people. It's a companion film to *Vice Squad,* leaving an even worse aftertaste.

Finally, there is the male whore, the professional lover who parlays his looks, build, charm, equipment and expertise into a cushy lifestyle; that is, if he has the smarts and the right connections. In real life there are a lot of them, especially teen hustlers, but screen portrayals have been scarce. Jon Voight caused a sensation with his naive Joe Buck in the originally X-rated *Midnight Cowboy* (1969), but its Academy Awards and commercial success did not encourage a trend toward screen gigolos.

Porno movies, both gay and straight, have offered lots of male whores, but the few mainstream portrayals have tended to emphasize extremes: a life of cushy affluence or one of struggle laden with soap-opera angst. Mathieur Carriere's character in *A Woman in Flames* is certainly well-off in addition to being attractive and charming, but he is getting old (he's in his thirties) and plans to use his savings to fund a restaurant.

Meanwhile, the 42nd Street hustlers in *Forty Deuce* (1985) have to contend with an OD'd male trick, a fascist pimp, drug dealers and a corrupt rich client. It can be a discouraging way of life at times.

One of the emptiest portrayals of a hustler is that of Richard Gere in *American Gigolo* (1981), a feature-length wish-fulfillment directed by Paul Schrader with

Richard Gere looks to be waiting for a sexual verdict from Lauren Hutton in American Gigolo *(1980).*

his customary fixation on technique over substance. Gere's primary function is to service upper-class Lauren Hutton, but Gere is so lacking in screen presence, star quality and simple humanity that you wonder why Hutton settles for him over a better-looking, more personable stud to fill her needs.

The commercial appeal of male prostitute roles, when they occur, is that they fulfill vicarious needs for male *and* female audiences. The men imagine themselves to be well-built studs paid to satisfy the pent-up desires of either older men or beautiful women, while the women swoon over the thought of a handsome, well-endowed pro bringing them to multiple climaxes.

Prostitutes of all kinds fulfill various fantasy needs in movies, which is why there are so many of them and will continue to be. Whether or not they are true to life is beside the point. The fact is that going to see movies involving prostitutes is cheaper than paying for the real thing, and if a famous actor or actress is playing the part, that only heightens the fantasy. So long as there *is* this double-edged value, movie screens will be dripping with ladies and gentlemen of the evening and the allure of naughty sex.

Chapter 5
STUDS, BITCHES AND FEMME FATALES

Jack Nicholson: "I don't think I fuck more than a dozen new girls a year now."
Art Garfunkel: "You can't make fucking your life's work."—from *Carnal Knowledge.*

"You shouldn't wear that body."—William Hurt to Kathleen Turner in *Body Heat.*

The opposite of sex to promote love and enhance intimacy is sex for manipulation and betrayal, the cunning craft of using sexual wiles to obtain power, wealth and revenge. Also to use people as objects for self-gratification or to prove one's manhood through erection and orgasm.

These are the *real* sins of sex in cinema and they have been with us since Theda Bara vamped her way through *A Fool There Was* in 1912. Sex in the movies, as in real life, is often a game of exploitation for ulterior motives. Movies since 1970 have, as always, provided a rich array of crafty, often villainous men and women for whom sex is a more potent weapon than a knife or a gun because it erodes the senses in slow, torturous degrees, inflicting a more lasting and awful punishment than mere physical death.

Before we go any further, let us define our terms. Though the stud is often a swinger and would seem to belong in Chapter 1, for the purposes of this discussion, the stud is one of four types: 1) He is an egotistic

sex machine who measures his self-worth solely in terms of conquest; 2) he is a hater of women who uses his manhood as a tool of revenge, which is often how type number one ends up; 3) he is a tool used by rich, powerful women—or *he* uses *them*—because he happens to have the right combination of looks, physique, prowess and stamina; or 4) he is a ladies' man who takes pleasure in one-night stands because he knows he's irresistible, but at the same time fears commitment because that means letting a woman get close to him, which is the *last* thing he wants. This latter type is typified by James Bond, who always gets entangled with a bitch or femme fatale for double trouble, but he can also be an ordinary macho guy who is sometimes plagued by self-doubt.

The bitch is a woman who uses wealth or techniques of domination to gain control/subservience of men. She is beautiful, wicked, demanding, haughty, arrogant, vengeful and murderous. A fireball of treachery and deceit who uses men for purely selfish or evil

ends. Screw once (or a few times) and throw away.

The femme fatale can also be a bitch, as in spy movies, but more often she is a temptress, a sultry poisoner of men's minds who uses intercourse to get a man to commit heinous deeds he would never contemplate if he was thinking with his brain instead of his genitals. In short, she is a vision of lust beckoning a man to self-destruction for *her* gain.

In the early 1970's, Jack Nicholson embodied both the stud as sex machine and as a misogynist in movies like *Five Easy Pieces* (1970) and *Carnal Knowledge* (1971). The former is a study of self-alienation and self-doubt in which sex is a means of proving that life has meaning if only during the moment of climax. The title, after all, can be taken as meaning sexual conquests.

Carnal Knowledge, though, is a scorching examination of the famous Four F approach to sex, which emphasizes scoring and performance over learning how to love a woman and cherish her as a human being, not just as a sex object. Nicholson's character doesn't see women as people, he sees them as things, judging them by their looks and bust size and their willingness to screw without making any demands on him as a person. If they do make demands, they are seen as ballbusters and castrators. Which is why Nicholson doesn't want to marry: marriage means commitment and demands and the loss of identity. When he does marry, he still screws around, growing increasingly contemptuous of modern women as demanding bitches until he ends up impotent, able to achieve erection only when enacting a pre-arranged reassuring scenario of macho virility with hooker Rita Moreno.

In Five Easy Pieces *(1970), Nicholson was both affectionate…*

…and passionate with girlfriend Karen Black.

In Carnal Knowledge *(1971), Nicholson had no problem using his sleazy brand of macho charm to score with coed Candice Bergen.*

But ended up marrying sexpot Ann-Margret for her build and breasts.

Inevitably, he paid for his attitude with misogynist impotence, compelling him to pay for sexual reassurance from prostitute Rita Moreno.

In Chinatown *(1975), Jack Nicholson gets involved with client Faye Dunaway while investigating a bizarre murder case.*

What this all adds up to is a dead-on, damning portrait of the stud mentality, an indictment of every man who thinks that women should feel honored to be impaled by such a superior cocksman, never realizing that most women view a man as more than a penis with a body attached. The stud's is a tragic tale indeed, and all one can do is pity him for his self-defeating, dead-end view of male-female relationships.

The same idea was put forth in *Fellini's Casanova* (1976), in which Donald Sutherland plays the title role to an enigmatic extreme, wearing some of the ugliest make-up ever conceived, making you wonder what women saw in this guy. It was Fellini's idea that by portraying this legendary lover as an unattractive, self-absorbed sex machine, we would end up feeling as disgusted as he. All the viewer ends up feeling, though, is cold and uninvolved.

Porno movies have also depicted stud types one and two with a vengeance, both prototypically played by John Leslie, who has made a career of playing the professional smartass seducer in movies like *The Story of Joanna* (1975), *Mary, Mary* (1977), *Talk Dirty to Me* (1980) and its sequel, *Nothing to Hide* (1982). In the first film, he plays a stud who vents hostility toward women with his penis and S&M, eventually going gay. In the second, he is given a perpetual erection by the Devil, becoming the ultimate satyr. In the latter two movies, he is *the* cocksure cocksman, viewing women only as objects for lustful conquest, betting retarded buddy, Richard Pacheco, in *Talk Dirty to Me,* that he can score with nymphomaniac Jessie St. James in three days. His is the classic Four F approach, boasting that any lady ain't never been laid like he can lay them, which in all cases turns out to be conventional in-and-out pumping, hardly arousing to most women in real life.

The exception to the rule in Leslie's output is the unusually artful and sensitive *Every Woman Has a Fantasy* (1984), in which Leslie's ladies' man is fascinated by the sexual fantasies his wife, Rachel Ashley, and her girlfriends discuss at their weekly get-togethers. Every time Leslie makes love in this movie, it's as though he cares as much about the woman's orgasm as his own, which is also rare for most porno movies. For a change, Leslie digs below the surface of his accustomed image to find the man behind the plumbing.

Stud type three has been depicted in movies like *Shampoo* (1975) and *The Stud* (1978). In the satiric *Shampoo,* Warren Beatty incorporates a bit of type four as a hairdressing satyr who hops in and out of several high-class beds in the course of one long, fatiguing day, parlaying his Rodeo Drive connections into what he hopes will be funding for the private hair salon he wants to open. He has the hots for Julie Christie (his former real-life lover), Lee Grant and Carrie Fisher (the latter two are mother and daughter taking turns with his body), while girlfriend Goldie Hawn wants him to settle down with her alone. Beatty seems to be flaunting his real-life reputation as a stud supreme as a man who complains about his sex-starved customers but who revels in satisfying their needs.

The Stud also involves a bitch, *the* bitch of the 70's and 80's: Joan Collins. Here, she plays a wealthy, adulterous nymphomaniac who sets up gigolo Oliver Tobias (who looks like Beatty, who was one of Collins's former lovers) in a life of tailored luxury in exchange for his well-endowed sexual services on demand, including a steamy scene in an elevator. When Tobias chucks Collins in disgust after failing to perform at an orgy for her friends, she turns on him by stripping him of the goodies and social status she gave him. The Stud promises a lot but delivers more

Donald Sutherland as Fellini's Casanova *(1976), even in scenes like this, in the arms of nun Margaret Clement, lacked erotic punch.*

Such is Warren Beatty's all-purpose charm in Shampoo *(1985) that he can seduce Lee Grant at a formal party while Julie Christie looks on without complaint.*

The premier movie and TV bitch of the late 70's through late 80's was sultry Joan Collins, here receiving a lustful command performance in an elevator courtesy of her kept lover Oliver Tobias in The Stud *(1978). (Courtesy of the Academy of Motion Picture Arts and Sciences)*

As James Bond, everyone's favorite one-man spy and sex machine, Roger Moore always got the girl, preferably in a reclining position. Here he is with Britt Ekland in The Man With the Golden Gun *(1974)...*

With Emily Bolton in Moonraker *(1979)...*

innuendo than action, at least in the American version. Collins reprised her role in an even worse movie *The Bitch* (1980), which even she detests. Her comments appear hypocritical because her sister, Jackie Collins, scripted both movies and she certainly knew what she was getting into, and for some good exposure (pun intended).

Stud type four, as mentioned earlier, comes in two categories: the professional spy à la James Bond, and the macho man whose life is a series of aimless sexual encounters. Bond, of course, is everyone's favorite one-man spy team/sex machine because he is handsome, suave, charming, witty, aggressive and great in bed. Part of the fun of the Bond films is watching Bond score with a variety of pretty women, some of them bitches/femme fatales. Or rather, it used to be fun. Until the rival Bond films of 1983, the women had increasingly become interchangeable faces and bodies to show that Bond still had sex appeal. Few of these women had any color or character to them, and you had to ask yourself how sexy any man is when you know he's going to score without half trying because it's *de rigueur* for the series.

Sean Connery is easily the most charismatic of the actors who have played Bond, not only because he created the role on screen, but because he's a fine actor, projects strength and decisiveness literally under fire, and simply has greater sexual presence than Roger Moore. Connery also has an ingratiating air of wry self-mockery, leavening his bed antics with humor. He doesn't seem to take his women for granted as Moore later did.

Though the best Bond films were the first three in the 1960's, Connery has also been fun to watch in *Diamonds are Forever* (1971), opposite and on top of tantalizing Jill St. John, and in the more recent *Never Say Never Again* (1983). Both movies are overlong, convoluted and pointless, though the latter has historical value because it brought back the Real Bond after too long an absence and gave him two new lovers: steamy knockout Kim Basinger with her full, pouty, sensuous lips and a body to rouse the dead, and bitch/femme fatale Barbara Carrera, a worthy adversary in and out of bed.

You have to admire a woman like Carrera who is so efficiently, ruthlessly evil, and who so casually wears a snake like a scarf while driving. She is also one bitch who gets so caught up in her own erotic self-image that in a moment of hysterical sexual egotism she tries to get Connery at gun point to admit she was his greatest lover. "Well," he replies tongue-in-cheek to infuriate her, "there *was* this girl in Philadelphia."

Roger Moore makes an adequate Bond, but he is less of a solid, versatile actor than Connery because his forte is light comedy, and most of the scripts written for him have reflected that. Moore's Bond films have also gotten increasingly silly, emphasizing special effects, high-priced gimmickry and female mannequins over strong plots, character development and a serious lover for Bond. You have to ask yourself why this aging spy, for all his debonair maturity, can never latch onto one good woman for very long; someone with as much to offer him as he can or is willing to offer in return. Moore appeared to have met his kindred ally in Maud Adams as the title character of *Octopussy* (1983), but you knew that unlike Bond, alas, she wouldn't be back. She was replaced by the stylized-looking Grace Jones in the pathetic *A View to a Kill* (1985). Jones is an actress with screen presence

but limited erotic appeal because of her butch appearance and masculine demeanor.

Stud type four as a selfish or aimless womanizer has been characterized in several films. In *Lifeguard* (1976), Sam Elliott as the thirtyish title character attracts women like a magnet because of his looks, build and shallow charm, but he has no feeling for them other than a sexual one, which is the secret of his success. When he meets his high school sweetheart (Anne Archer) at a class reunion, there is an air of seriousness that makes him want to shy away as he did once before with her. Some men are afraid to grow up.

Richard Gere in *Looking for Mr. Goodbar* (1977) and *Breathless* (1981) plays a cocky bar stud and an amoral wise-ass on-the-loose respectively. His general

But for everyone else, there will always be only one James Bond: dynamically masculine Sean Connery. Here he makes steamy love to bitch/femme fatale Barbara Carrera in his 007 comeback film, Never Say Never Again *(1983).*

This publicity pose of Richard Gere and Valerie Kaprisky for Breathless (1983) is steamier than anything shown in the movie.

This clinch by Sonia Braga and Jose Wilker in Dona Flor and Her Two Husbands *(1981) seems to be the real thing.*

Sam Elliott in the title role of Lifeguard *(1975) shares a moment of post-coital uncertainty with Sharon Weber.*

In the TV movie For Ladies Only *(1979), Gregory Harrison displayed mature hunk appeal as a disco stripper known as Zorro. (Courtesy U.S.A. Home Video)*

attitude is that women should be grateful to get it on with a dude like him, but when pressed for details as to who and what he is, he backs off, and that's the problem. It's also a problem that Gere is so obnoxious in these films you wonder why any woman would be drawn to him other than because the script says so.

Two other stud films bear comparison because they deal with the same subject: the stud or near-stud as male stripper, flaunting his body and magnetism before hundreds of screaming, sex-starved women at a discotheque. Christopher Atkins in *A Night in Heaven* (1983) is dripping with animal allure as he strips to the waist in front of his speech teacher Lesley Ann Warren who has just flunked him. He is simultaneously adorable and menacing, the stud as youthful sex god who knows he can have any woman on earth just by grinning and winking in her direction. Away from the disco, the movie is flat, empty and dull because there is no strong storyline to add to the excitement of the disco scenes; there is only a softcore sex scene with Atkins and Warren that is laughably ludicrous for its semi-explicit writhings.

The TV movie *For Ladies Only* (1980) is far superior in every respect because it has a strong script and its characters have dimension and meaningful goals; in this case a Broadway acting career. Here Gregory Harrison falls into the role of stud when he takes a job at a ladies disco strip joint, first as a semi-nude waiter, then as a star attraction strip dancer who drives women wild.

The conflict here is between integrity and whoring, or rather types of whoring. On the one hand, Harrison refuses to service high-powered businesswoman Lee Grant in exchange for her underwriting his acting career, but leaps at the chance to make a fortune by whoring his fame as New York's leading male stripper in exchange for a Broadway break. At least Grant's offer was a discreet one and wouldn't have biased Broadway showmen against him on sight. Either way, Harrison is offered a choice as to the most profitable use of his looks and body and ends up making the wrong decision.

The major difference between the two films is that *For Ladies Only* uses Harrison's hunkish masculine appeal as the basis for a full and satisfying story in which the characters evolve and change for the better, with an underlying moral, whereas *A Night in Heaven* tries to dodge by on a few minutes of flashing lights, piercing screams and a male lead who's cute but shallow.

Lest we forget the women in this discussion, there is one other, important femme fatale from the early 80's: Kathleen Turner as the siren of doom in *Body Heat* (1981), one of the most erotic mainstream American movies of the last ten years.

All eyes are on sexually magnetic nightclub stripper Christopher Atkins in A Night in Heaven (1983), except for Leslie Ann Warren, who shies away from his undulating advances while sister Deborah Rush looks on.

Sultry siren Kathleen Turner became one of the hottest sex stars of the early 80's when she wove her lustful web of passion, deceit and murder to ensnare William Hurt in the sizzlingly erotic Body Heat *(1981). Once she had her man, she could be either quietly concerned about the two of them (Courtesy Landmark Theatres)…*

The script by Lawrence Kasdan (who also wrote *Raiders of the Lost Ark)* combines the plots of *Double Indemnity* and *The Postman Always Rings Twice,* nearly outstripping the original film versions of each, certainly outshining the remake of the latter that same year. This is not merely because Kasdan didn't have to pull any erotic punches but because he conjured a better narrative and cast leading actors who created a powerful sexual chemistry between them.

That is the major difference between the censored originals and the steamy update: that the sexual attraction between femme fatale Turner and horny patsy William Hurt could be more open and explicit while still retaining an R rating because the action is framed and edited to arouse an audience while leaving a great deal to the imagination. In fact, one of the sexiest scenes shows no action at all. Turner and Hurt have just had a bout, he gets up to look out the window and she grabs him by his peniş to lead him around the room. It's sexy because it's playfully aggressive.

What Turner adds to the role of female predator is both a modern sensibility and a more open, naked passion for her victim. Even as she is setting him up for the inevitable fall, her desire for him is genuine, to the point of risking exposure while fellating him in the outdoors at her home. Her performance is a knockout.

...or burning with desire for his body.

Turner went on to spoof her *Body Heat* image in the misfired Steve Martin comedy *The Man with Two Brains* (1983), then had more big hits in the rousing adventure movie *Romancing the Stone* (1984), its silly sequel *The Jewel of the Nile* (1985), and the slow-paced, overpraised *Godfather* parody, *Prizzi's Honor* (1985). In the latter, she plays a Mafia contract killer as femme fatale, snaring and manipulating dim-witted Jack Nicholson. Whatever else she does for encores in a movie career assured of a very long run, film history will record Turner for two prize achievements: for being a vamp who could arouse a dead man, and for being one of our most memorably uninhibited wicked women of the screen, in the tradition of and in a league with the likes of Barbara Stanwyck, Rita Hayworth and Joan Collins.

Blonde sexpot Cheri Caffaro is bandoleered for action as a female James Bond called Ginger in The Abductors *(1972). (Courtesy I.V.E. Home Video)*

Demonically possessed Sigourney Weaver in Ghostbusters (1984) surprises nerdy neighbor Rick Moranis with her suddenly voluptuous availability. (Courtesy Peter H. Brown)

Kiss of the Spiderwoman (1985): In the melodramatic movie within the movie, chanteuse fatale Sonia Braga betrays the French resistance for love of Nazi officer Herson Capri. (Courtesy Island Pictures)

Jazz musi-cian Richard Gere takes a chance with his life during a gig at The Cotton Club *(1984) by succumb-ing to the sultry charm of gangster's moll Diane Lane.*

As the wanton title seductress in Bizet's
Carmen *(1984), Julia Migenes-Johnson has
soldier Placido Domingo torn between his
duty and her bed. Is there really any
competition?*

The gallery of studs, bitches and femme fatales
discussed here incluudes both realistic characteriza-
tions and cartoon variations on a theme. Men and
women we can either identify with or root for and hiss
at. What we carry away from the verité likenesses and
the broad caricatures depends, of course, on what we
wish to carry away, but there can certainly be no doubt
that movies of the 70's and 80's have given us more to
think about and reflect on regarding our treatment of
each other in real life. We can see the consequences of
regarding people as objects for gratification or manipulation, but we can also see that sex can, should and
must involve genuine responsiveness and commitment if we are to form relationships based on love and
respect rather than hurt and betrayal.

(Top and left) Variety *(1984): By day, Sandy
McLeod is a cashier at a Times Square
porno theatre.*

*By night she fancies herself a femme fatale
in the mold of a porn star by dressing in
slinky lingerie. (Courtesy Bette Gor-
don/Horizon Films)*

Chapter 6
DRAG QUEENS AND ROLE REVERSALS

"I was a better man with you as a woman than I ever was with a woman as a man. I just gotta learn to do it without the dress."—Dustin Hoffman to Jessica Lange in *Tootsie*.

Drag acts are as old as show business, dating back hundreds of years to medieval times when women were not allowed on stage because acting was not considered a ladylike profession, forcing men to play female roles. The women in all of Shakespeare's plays were originally played by men for that very reason, and it was only much later that Juliet, Kate, Portia and Lady Macbeth all spoke with natural soprano tones.

Drag in modern times has become more of a comic novelty, the camp value of seeing a man in woman's clothing. Milton Berle made a career of drag shtick on his legendary live TV show in the 40's and 50's; in the 1960's, Flip Wilson was hilariously bitchy—and sexy—as Geraldine, and Jonathan Winters was a crotchety delight as Maude Frickert; the Monty Python troup took turns in drag both for laughs and because they rarely used a woman in their act; the 1980-82 TV series *Bosom Bodies* took its cue from *Some Like it Hot* by having Peter Scolari and Tom Hanks doll up so they

could share a room at an all-female rooming house; Terry Sweeney has made a name for himself with his drag impersonations on "Saturday Night Live"; and entertainers like Canada's Craig Russell have their gay audiences howling with delight at impersonations of homosexuals' favorites such as Judy Garland, Joan Crawford and Tallulah Bankhead.

If you want to analyze it, drag is a means of violating accepted sexual images and stereotypes, of seeing how well a man can behave as a woman, bringing out his feminine side. This is certainly what intrigues women who find drag acts amusing and is clearly what appeals to homosexuals, though many straight men are mystified by its appeal as entertainment.

For the purpose of this chapter, I am discussing drag both as a comic device and as a serious means of examining male/female role reversals; how changing one's sexual identity can alter and expand one's view

Tim Curry is that campy, flashy "transvestite from transsexual Transylvania" in the outrageous cult classic The Rocky Horror Picture Show *(1975). (Courtesy Landmark Theatres)*

of life and the opposite sex by literally or almost literally becoming that sex.

In movies, as in real life, drag comes in two types: the transvestite (literally "cross dresser"), a man who dresses up either to entertain others or because he feels more comfortable wearing women's clothes (female transvestites are not so common); and the transsexual, the man or woman who literally changes his or her sex through surgery. Few movies have dealt with the latter since 1970 because it's a risky subject lacking mass commercial appeal.

The most sensationalistic of the small group of films about transsexuals is the biographical *The Christine Jorgensen Story* (1970), which ineptly and exploitatively told the tale of how a man named George Jorgensen (John Hansen) became the world's first person to change his sex through complicated surgery which involves using the penis to form a vagina and clitoris. The real Jorgensen was interviewed for actress Lee Grant's documentary on transvestites and transsexuals, *What Sex Am I?* (1985).

There has also been the misfired *Myra Breckenridge* (1970), in which Rex Reed miraculously became Raquel Welch (this one also obviously involved extensive plastic and vocal surgery), who was bent on dominating men, especially through anal rape. And there was the British film *I Want What I Want* (1972), in which Anne Heywood played a young man disguised as a woman who undergoes surgery for a permanent change because he feels more at ease as a woman. Some critics viewed this as a movingly unsensationalistic saga about the dual nature of masculine/feminine identity, while others saw it as a slow, labored and pretentious soap opera of little value in which Heywood was unconvincing in her male role. It has not been seen in the U.S. since its original release.

Another woman who played a man was Linda Hunt in *The Year of Living Dangerously* (1983), but here the casting was not a ploy for novelty but to hire the right actor to play a midget Indonesian photographer/middleman. Hunt is technically fine in the role (she won an Oscar for it), but the knowledge that it's a woman playing a man detracts from its overall effectiveness.

The most charming and definitive transsexual character of them all was John Lithgow's ex-football player in *The World According to Garp* (1982). The script, direction and acting do not feel uneasy about or poke fun at transsexuality, but imbue the character with humor, dignity and compassion, and accept the fact that this is a human being who changed course in life, is happier and more content for it, and is certainly no less a delightful person to be around. Lithgow practically steals the show with his breakthrough performance.

Transsexual Anne Heywood in I Want What I Want *(1972) faces the wrath of uptight dad Harry Andrews for preferring to dress and live as a woman.*

John Lithgow stole the show in The World According to Garp *(1982) as a former football player literally turned woman. Here, he comforts Robin Williams as Garp, one friend to another.*

Female impersonator George Sanders in The Kremlin Letter *(1970) has got to be the ugliest* drag queen *of all time.*

For the rest of the 70's, plain old drag was in vogue, almost always as a sight gag. George Sanders played an aging queen in *The Kremlin Letter* (1970); gay prisoner Michael Greer did a bitchy drag act for his fellow inmates in the abysmally exploitative *Fortune and Men's Eyes* (1971); Burt Reynolds and Jack Weston dressed as nuns to catch some crooks in *Fuzz* (1972); Lou Jacobi made an improbable middle-aged Jewish transvestite in *Everything You Always Wanted to Know About Sex* (1972); Diana Rigg joined Vincent Price in bobby guise in the horror comedy *Theatre of Blood* (1973); Jeff Bridges made himself pretty for a con job in *Thunderbolt and Lightfoot* (1974); Jerry Stiller was tossed out of a gay bathhouse in drag in *The Ritz* (1976); Marlon Brando donned a bonnet and calico dress to spy on Jack Nicholson in *The Missouri Breaks* (1976); and Walter Matthau found himself forced to dress in a skirt and scarf to make his way home in *House Calls* (1978). Most of these bits were no more than a throwaway or extended bit of business designed to give an extra comic shot in the arm, usually in a movie that needed it.

Walter Matthau in House Calls *(1978) checks to see if anyone has spotted him in his ersatz drag get-up.*

(Right) Gay convict Michael Greer does a campy drag act for the entertainment of his fellow inmates in Fortune and Men's Eyes *(1971).*

(Below) Diana Rigg and Vincent Price look jolly good as phony bobbies in their pursuit of yet another know-it-all drama critic in Theatre of Blood *(1973).*

Burt Reynolds and Jack Weston in Fuzz *(1972) are understandably apprehensive sitting around in nuns' habits waiting to bait a crook.*

(Left) Has Clint Eastwood gone gay all of a sudden? No, he's just discussing the details of a robbery with crooked cohort Jeff Bridges, who is dressed in drag as part of the scheme in Thunderbolt and Lightfoot *(1974).*

The most popular drag acts of the 70's were Divine (neé Harris Milstead) in *Pink Flamingos* (1972), Tim Curry in *The Rocky Horror Picture Show* (1975), and Michel Serrault in *La Cage aux Folles* (1978). The first two movies made cult stars of Divine and Curry. Divine played a revolting travesty of a "woman" in *Pink Flamingos,* vying for the role of "world's filthiest human being" by devouring a plateful of dog crap in the final reel. Curry, on the other hand, outrageously vamped his campy way through *Rocky Horror,* stealing a bizarre show as a corseted and rouged mad doctor who creates his own handmade Adonis and makes love to an engaged straight couple. He knows no shame as he cavorts with flashy style and a wicked, lipsmacking gleam.

A chorus line of male and female drag queens in The Rocky Horror Picture Show. *Note the golden oldie logo they're cavorting in front of.*

Michel Serrault (left) in La Cage aux Folles *(1979) faces up to the fact one of his transient studs doesn't have the talent to pass muster with lover/cabaret owner Ugo Tognazzi (middle).*

La Cage aux Folles was the biggest mainstream success of the three, with Serrault as an aging cabaret drag queen whose constant fits of prima donna fury send club owner and lover Ugo Tognazzi right up the wall. Instead of creating a patronizing caricature, Serrault enveloped his character with warmth, dignity, affection and the sense that he enjoys being what he is: a homosexual who dresses like a woman to make a

living, and who revels in giving his effeminacy free rein within that professional context. It's a consummate comic performance and a wonderful one.

Also wonderful was Craig Russell more or less playing himself in Richard Benner's *Outrageous!* (1977). The twist here is that by impersonating Judy and Joan and Tallulah and all the other gay camp "faves," Russell feels in touch with their spirits. He is a

Dustin Hoffman as soap opera star Dorothy Michaels in Tootsie *(1982) rejects a lecherous come-on by co-star George Gaynes…*

…but is genuinely touched by the heartfelt wooing of Charles Durning, the father of Jessica Lange, with whom Hoffman is really in love.

gay man on the outside, but a woman at heart inside, paying attention to all those crazy voices in his head because they give his life meaning and sustenance. They enable him as well to understand the inner torment of a schizophrenic female (Hollis McLaren) whose mental voices make it impossible for her to cope with reality. The ending is a sentimental cop-out for that reason: Russell tells McLaren there is nothing to worry about because he too hears voices when he should be seeking more competent medical help for her than she has been getting. Still, the point is well made that "all the best people are a little crazy inside"; some people are just more in touch with their craziness than others.

The gloomiest, most Kafkaesque role reversal of the 70's was Roman Polanski's in his own *The Tenant* (1976), in which he plays a meek, obsequious clerk who becomes possessed by the spirit of a mad woman who killed herself in the apartment he now occupies. Polanski was obviously aiming for a fraught-with-meaning psychological horror story about dual personalities, but his thematic intent is swamped in unrelieved dourness and pseudo-symbolism for their own sake at the expense of a sharply compelling narrative and a character transformation we can care about. The poor little guy is such a diffident oddball to begin with, is it any surprise when he takes on a dead woman's personality and goes insane with it?

So far in the 1980's, there have been only two high-flying drag queen/role reversal movies: *Tootsie* and *Victor/Victoria.* Both are comedies, both were released in 1982, both challenged stereotypical notions of sexual role playing. Though *Tootsie* was the more commercially successful of the two because of all the hype about Dustin Hoffman doing a star turn in drag and because it was a feminist cause célèbre, it is less successful in terms of character development and themes, despite very witty writing and direction.

In *Tootsie,* Dustin Hoffman hoaxes the entire American public by masquerading as a woman on network television. As Dorothy Michaels, Hoffman supposedly learns more about being a woman and the female side of his own psyche, potentially becoming more adept at and sensitive to male/female relations. But does he really? He gets the job on the soap opera by aggressively belieing the prettily made-up Southern belle image he has adopted to land the role, proving that a woman can look soft but act tough when she needs to. So far so good, though it's hard to believe that anyone in real life would be convinced that Hoffman's Dorothy Michael is really a woman: the voice he uses is not believably female.

Next he goes on to revamp the melodramatic drivel he is given to perform by ad libbing the hell out of it, making not only his own character but the entire show more plausible and dynamically spontaneous, boosting it higher in the ratings. But, rather than pursue the one intelligent woman who is genuinely interested in him as a man, Teri Garr, he lusts after the soap opera's affectionate but bubble-headed co-star Jessica Lange, who says she is looking for an honest, sensitive man, but is dating the deceitful, chauvinistic director of the soap opera, Dabney Coleman. Here is where the movie gets into problems.

First of all, when Hoffman tells Lange at a party what she herself said would turn her on to a man, namely a direct but sincere sexual proposal, she tosses a drink in his face. This is meant to be funny because it makes her out a hypocrite and him still the aggressive macho male. All it really makes you think is doesn't she recognize her own fantasy approach when confronted with it? Secondly, when Hoffman accepts an invitation to spend a weekend with Lange and her father, Charles Durning, in the country, he shares Lange's bed. This is incredible in the extreme because it assumes that a) Hoffman's wig won't slip off during the night; b) that he won't get an erection; and c) that Lange won't accidentally flop over him during the night and discover his secret. The drag act would certainly be literally uncovered in that circumstance. Or didn't that occur to screenwriters Larry Gelbart and Murray Schisgal?

Next, we are supposed to think it's funny that Charles Durning has fallen in love with Dorothy because we know what he doesn't, but how can you feel superior to a man whose only "crime" is being romantically human? As for the movie being a blow for feminine equality and independence because Hoffman becomes more sensitized, it is nothing of the sort. In the process of courting Lange as Dorothy, he neglects and degrades Garr, letting her think he's gay. And when he wins Lange in the end, it is not because of his vaunted new sensitivity, regardless of the quote at the top of this chapter, but because he is aggressively pursuing her. His sexual chauvinism and taste for passive women remain unchanged and likewise her attraction to aggressive, deceitful men is bolstered. He may be more articulate in handing a woman a good line, but he is still the same pseudo-sincere heel he's always been. The audience may think he's come a long way, but his death toll of broken hearts shows only that he was successful at fooling people, not in elevating his knowledge of or dealings with them. The only thing he has proven is that he can play a woman better than a woman and get away with it until his lust for Lange compels him to unmask himself.

Some feminist statement.

By comparison, *Victor/Victoria* is not only better entertainment but far more thematically honest. It is

Dustin Hoffman beautifully dressed as the All-American Woman in Tootsie *(1982), backed by that Grand Old Flag.*

Gay cabaret entertainer Robert Preston instructs Julie Andrews in the fine points of behaving like a man in Victor/Victoria *(1982).*

But it's "Le Jazz Hot," baby, when it comes time to strut her stuff as a female impersonator.

also a rare instance of double drag: destitute singer Julie Andrews is persuaded by gay cabaret performer Robert Preston to become a female impersonator by cutting her hair, dressing in men's clothes á la George Sand, and lowering her voice á la Noel Coward (by way of Daniel Massey in *Star*), to pull off the hoax. When James Garner is seduced by her stage performance but learns that Andrews is a "man," he has to convince himself it's a woman in disguise because his macho male ego won't tolerate the thought of bisexual attraction.

Garner's gut feeling that Andrews is really a woman underscores the movie's major drawback: that Andrews is no more convincing as a man than Dustin Hoffman is as a woman. Not only is the voice an affected giveaway, but Andrews facially doesn't *look* masculine even with her hair shorn. But then, Tony Curtis and Jack Lemmon weren't convincing as women either in Billy Wilder's *Some Like it Hot.*

Nevertheless, you can go along with the make-believe of *Victor/Victoria* for the same reasons Billy Wilder was able to suspend disbelief with his classic drag farce: the script is witty (though not as razor-sharp as it could have been), the performances are almost all first-rate—especially Robert Preston's—and Blake Edwards's direction is polished and relaxed, though he could have taken a few more lessons on the art of sly sexual comedy from Wilder and Ernst Lubitsch, since a few scenes come off awkward or forced. Overall, Edwards induces thought as well as laughter, scoring some riotous comic points about male/female roles and how it is no disgrace or shame to embrace both sides of oneself or to admit either bisexuality or homosexuality.

Also, unlike *Tootsie,* the title character doesn't dump on one would-be lover in pursuit of another, then call herself sensitive, but plays a titillating game of hide-sex-and-go-seek, ending jubilantly in the final reel with Andrews snaring a happier, and wiser, Garner. The topper is Preston doing a production number in the final reel in which he is one of the *ugliest* drag queens of all time, *and* the most marvelously inept. He alone is worth the price of admission.

The Monty Python troop cross dresses for their evening meal in Monty Python's The Meaning of Life *(1983). Left to right they are Graham Chapman, Michael Palin (charming blouse), Terry Gilliam, Eric Idle (very tasteful), and Terry Jones (nondescript). That's John Cleese, center, as Death, dressed in what looks like an oversized Hefty trash bag.*

In Lust in the Dust *(1985), cult drag queen Divine (real name Harris Milstead) lurched out of the sewer cinema of John Waters into the comic mainstream. Here he vies with Lainie Kazan for the sexual attention of Tab Hunter. The real question here is why Hunter would be attracted to Divine in the first place.*

What we come away with from movies like *The World According to Garp, Outrageous!* and *Victor/Victoria* is that we all have a masculine and a feminine side, but that too many of us go to great lengths to cover up or deny that fact. Women are no less feminine for asserting themselves and men are no less masculine for displaying tender feelings. If movies can help us tap these aspects of ourselves in positive, productive ways, then they have fulfilled their obligations both as art and inspiration.

From left to right Jonathan Prince, Michael Zorek and Matthew Modine in Private School *(1983) think they can drag their way into the girls' dorm, but they aren't fooling anyone, least of all Betsy Russell.*

Chapter 7
INCEST

"Incest has relatively little to do with sex. What these men yearn for, most of them, is comfort, warmth, security, intimacy, love."—Kevin Conway in *Something About Amelia.*

"The moral consideration is that it's a horrifying thought, and it's a horrifying thought because it always has been. Biologically speaking I'd say there's nothing wrong with it. Nothing."—From Theodore Sturgeon's short science-fiction story "If All Men Were Brothers, Would You Let One Marry Your Sister?"

The moral code that forbids sex between relatives, especially between parents and children, dates back thousands of years. It is one of the dominant social proscriptions of every known culture, western and otherwise. Playwrights from Sophocles to Eugene O'Neill have devoted whole plays to the subject, the most famous of which is Sophocles' *Oedipus the King,* taken from the classic Greek myth of a king who is damned for killing his father and marrying his mother. Though the tragedy of Oedipus is a morally symbolic one, it does have a bearing on incest as a modern, literal dilemma.

There are two main reasons for this dilemma, why incest is a social taboo. The primary concern is trauma, the anxiety that children who have sex with their parents will form an unnatural emotional attachment to them or, more often, will be scarred by the experience, either from the sheer terror of sexual contact or the sadistic abuse that might accompany it

or both. The fact that sexual molestation of children has risen dramatically in the U.S. in recent years serves to confirm these fears, especially in light of the McMartin Pre-School case in Los Angeles, the alleged Satanic ritual videotaped murders of three children in Sacramento, and the scandal in Scott County, Minnesota. More on these incidents later in this chapter.

This concern over trauma has naturally been escalating in print. An unsigned article in the April 14, 1980, issue of *Time* magazine bitterly took note of the then trend among sex researchers to undermine the incest taboo by asking what is wrong with familial sex in the first place. Both pro and con sides of the issue were raised, though the article's writer questions a child's ability to "produce anything like informed consent to an adult it depends on for life and guidance," contending that "the lifting of the incest barrier would invite the routine exploitation of children by disturbed parents."

The tender aftermath of mother-son incest in Louis Malle's landmark Murmur of the Heart *(1971). Lea Massari and Benoit Ferreux are the mother and child. (Courtesy Landmark Theatres)*

The secondary fear relating to incest is that it will produce congenitally defective children. In the story quoted above, Theodore Sturgeon provocatively addresses this fear, using livestock breeding as an analogy. He notes that animal relatives are mated to keep a strain going "until the desirable trait shows up recessive, and you stop it there. But it might never show up recessive. In any case, it's rare indeed when anything goes wrong in the very first generation. … And are you prepared to say that every mental retard is the product of an incestuous union? You'd better not, or you'll hurt the feelings of some pretty nice people." Of course this begs the question of whether the human race would want to or should interbreed given the chance, and the analogy is a specious one to begin with because you don't breed people like cattle or for the same reasons. Sturgeon's main point, though, is that we take this taboo for granted without thinking it through or questioning its social and sexual validity.

In the middle of all this heated debate are movies about or touching on incest. It used to be that under the Hays Code, even mentioning it was forbidden, but since the 1960's it has provided all kinds of dramatic fodder for filmmakers, some more serious than others. Nearly 80 movies explored the subject in the 60's, with or without the blessing of the Code and after it was abolished, while a couple of dozen more since 1970 have examined its emotional and psychological consequences.

Movies of the late 60's about incest often viewed it either in luridly melodramatic terms, as in *My Lover, My Son* (1970), which had a reverse Oedipal twist to it (the mother kills the father for love of the son), or as the path to perversity, as in *Goodbye Gemini* (1970), which told the story of a pair of incestuous twins with a taste for murder and kinky sex.

It wasn't until Louis Malle's notorious *Murmur of the Heart* (1971) that incest was viewed in a more rational light. Not as the product of a sick parental desire, but as a bond of love between mother and son, both of whom are shown to be normal, intelligent people, though the boy has a heart murmur (hence the title). The incest Malle implicitly shows is both inevitable and absolutely untraumatic; not the end of the world, but the humorous result of mutual loneliness and need, an incident not to be regretted but not to be repeated either. Because it does show that incest can happen beautifully and matter-of-factly, provoking serious thought about the subject either way, and also because it dramatizes or laughs at other sexual issues openly and cleanly, *Murmur of the Heart* is one of the healthiest movies ever made about human sexuality.

The most powerful American movie of the 70's with an incestual subtheme was *Chinatown* (1974), in which private eye Jack Nicholson literally slaps the

Wild-eyed Martin Potter kisses his twin sister/lover Judy Geeson in Goodbye Gemini *(1970) before strangling her.*

Romy Schneider seductively comes on to revolted son Dennis Waterman in My Lover, My Son *(1970) after she has murdered her husband/his father.*

Private eye Jack Nicholson in Chinatown *(1974) slaps the truth out of Faye Dunaway about her incestuous affair with father John Huston and the daughter/sister she had by him.*

truth out of Faye Dunaway about her relationship with her father, John Huston: that she bore him a daughter who of course is also her sister. This revelation shockingly underscores Huston's character of a greedy landowner/developer, a man who knows no morality when it comes to amassing ill-gotten riches or satisfying his lust. The ends always justify the means in his mind so long as he can get away with it.

Brian DePalma used the potential for incest in *Obsession* (1976), but only to rip off Alfred Hitchcock's *Vertigo.* Instead of a private detective who becomes mentally unbalanced in his attempt to remake one woman in the image of another, we have a mundane narrative about a businessman (Cliff Robertson) who falls in love with a young woman who is the exact double of his late wife, who was murdered by kidnappers. Only it turns out to be his daughter (both are played by Genevieve Bujold, making the entire movie transparent and obvious), who managed to escape her mother's fate. Except for the finale, when the camera

Cliff Robertson in Obsession *(1976) falls madly in love with pretty Genevieve Bujold, not knowing she's his long lost daughter whom he has presumed to be dead for many years.*

waltzes around the reunited father and daughter, *Obsession* is a shallow exercise in style over story, whereas Hitchcock used the former to tell and underscore the latter.

Bernardo Bertolucci tried to follow in Malle's cinematic footsteps with *Luna* (1979), the story of an American opera star (Jill Clayburgh) who moves to Italy with her drug addict son. She then initiates an affair with him that begins with masturbation to distract his need for drugs. This sounds intriguing but the movie fails as a potent commentary on incest where *Murmur of the Heart* succeeds because Bertolucci has an overbearing, ponderous touch, whereas Malle had a lightly humorous one. Moreover, Clayburgh plays her character with overbearing *joie de vivre,* while Matthew Barry as her druggie son is an annoying drudge.

In the late 70's, incest came to porno films, but more for its dirty-minded box-office appeal than because porn producers had anything to say about it. The first major movie to break the taboo was called *Taboo* (1980), starring Kay Parker as a divorcee whose need for male companionship drives her into an affair with her handsome son, Mike Ranger. She agonizes over what has happened (Parker gives a very good performance), but in the end implies she didn't think it was so bad and is going to keep the affair going.

Taboo was such a commercial hit because of its controversial theme that *Taboo II* followed a year later, this time featuring wall-to-wall orgiastic incest and no second thoughts about the right or wrong of it. *Taboo III* was released in 1984, again making piles of money (especially on home video). This time, Parker is duped by son number two (Jerry Butler) into sex thinking it's favorite son number one. Though there is some attempt in the first and third *Taboo* films to make a modicum of comment about the emotional and moral implications of incest, the emphasis is always on hardcore sex for its own sake. Parker says that porno producers "cannot afford to get too serious on the subject for fear of losing their audience. Acting in all three films has certainly given *me* cause to reflect upon the subject and I will hasten to state that I do not advocate or condone incest. At least these films, by their very existence, have people talking about a subject that used to be unmentionable in polite circles, and there is something to be said for that."

Other porn films with an incest theme include *Plato's the Movie* (1980), in which an obnoxious young man has anal sex with his mother in the fantasy room of a notorious swinger's club; and *A Scent of Heather* (1981), which is about a case of mistaken near-incest, told in the manner of a 1930's pulp gothic romance; and *Taboo American Style* (1985-86), which relates an

Jill Clayburgh in Luna *(1979) tenderly clutches son Matthew Marry to her bosom while contemplating the consequences of their incestuous affair.*

The incestuous cast of Taboo III *(1984): Mom Kay Parker (left), son/lover Jerry Butler (middle), and Honey Wilder (sitting), who is carrying on with her own son. (Courtesy Kay Parker)*

*Sorceress Morgana (Helen Mirren)
sends her evil son Mordred (Robert Addie)
forth to slay her half-brother and his father,
King Arthur, so that they can claim the
throne of England in the name of iniquity
in* Excalibur *(1981).*

ongoing saga of father-daughter/mother-son/brother-sister incest. Again, as with the *Taboo* films, these porn movies use incest as a plot device for as many hardcore sex scenes as can be squeezed into 90 minutes.

The one movie to use the Arthurian legends for an incestual subtheme was John Boorman's ravishingly produced *Excalibur* (1981), which deployed the Oedipus myth in reverse with a twist. Unlike other, more innocent movies based on Sir Thomas Mallory's *Le Morte d'Arthur,* such as *Camelot* which omits mention of incest, *Excalibur* is sexually aware and richly erotic for it. For the first time, a mainstream

fantasy film implicitly shows how the sorceress Morgan le Fay (Helen Mirren) bewitches her half-brother, King Arthur (Nigel Terry), into siring a bastard son named Mordred, who, in turn, is commanded by Morgana to slay his father and claim the throne of England. This incestual factor adds to the movie's dramatic tone and complexity with its subtext of disruptive evil versus idealistic, kingly good.

By far the strangest movie of the 80's to use incest was Tony Richardson's adaptation of John Irving's *The Hotel New Hampshire* (1984), which also had homosexuality, lesbianism, Marxist terrorism, a bear and a flatulent dog mixed into an indigestible, bizarre stew. Incest is depicted here in a joyfully ironic way: Brother and sister Rob Lowe and Jodie Foster are both homosexual. Nevertheless, they have desire for each other and in one triumphantly elliptical sequence, they expend their sibling lust, getting it out of their system but having fun doing it. Not only does this incest not traumatize them, it brings them closer together.

Other American movies in the 80's used incest either as a plot device or as a last-minute revelation intended to give the movie overall a more profound thematic reverberation, à la Rosebud in *Citizen Kane.* Incest as plot device was used in Steven Spielberg's *The Color Purple* (1985) to briefly sketch in the relationship between young Celie (Desreta Jackson) and her brutish stepfather as a setup for her marriage to an even more brutish black farmer. Any darker implications—such as what motivates the stepfather to incest—are sidestepped.

Incest as Rosebud is used in Robert Altman's *Fool for Love* (1985), which spends most of its boring running time showing estranged lovers Sam Shepard and Kim Basinger feudin' and fightin' before letting on that they are brother and sister. Since the movie up to that point has given us no reason to give a damn about this ongoing love feud in the first place—the dialogue and exposition are so minimal that the characters are empty—any hint at or mention of incest is beside the point, if there is one.

New Zealand's *Heart of the Stag* (1983) is a more direct and honest incest drama and one of the few discussed in this chapter which contain scenes of explicit incestual sex. The story is about a gruff, secretive, widowed sheep rancher (Terence Cooper) who has molested his daughter since she was a child, has regular sex with her as a woman (Mary Regan), and who becomes ragingly jealous of a stranger who is stealing her affection. For such a provocative story, *Heart of the Stag* is a sleeper: quiet rather than explosive for most of its dramatic effects. The low-key tone compels the viewer to sympathize with Regan's plight, to feel sorry that she is a secretive brooder like her father, and a virgin in relation to other men because she feels married to her father. Unfortunately, the script never bothers to explain what happened to the mother or why the father started preferring his daughter sexually. All we are given are brief hints in flashback, and that's not enough. Moreover, the ending is a cheat because instead of a final father-daughter-lover confrontation that puts the father in his place, Cooper is conveniently gored to death by a stag (symbolizing, I suppose, his animalistic machismo), letting him off the hook dramatically and robbing the viewer of catharsis and insight.

Fool for Love *(1985): Sultry Kim Basinger entwines with roving lover Sam Shepard just before kneeing him in the groin and over an hour before we learn they are actually brother and sister.*

New Zealand sheep rancher Terence Cooper grabs daughter Mary Regan in a fit of jealous rage in Heart of the Stag *(1983) when he suspects he might be losing her to another man.*

The most important film of the 80's about incest is the critically acclaimed, astronomically rated TV movie *Something About Amelia* (1984), written by William Handley and directed by Randa Haines. It was important for several reasons: 1) It dealt with a crucial, timely subject that television had previously avoided like the

Dressed and posed in their Sunday best, Ted Danson, Glenn Close, Olivia Cole and Rxana Zal look like the Amer-ican Dream come true in Something About Amelia *(1984).*

plague; 2) it dispelled the myth that incest is usually a drunken father attacking a seductive teenage daughter by presenting its story in the context of a normal American family; 3) it handled its touchy subject with maturity, taste, unpatronizing sensitivity and dramatic strength; and 4) it drew one of the largest audiences of all time for a TV movie, partly because of the subject, partly because of hype, partly because of rave reviews.

For the first time, a mass audience was drawn into the complex emotional and legal issues raised by incest. We are shown that what happens in such cases is that the accusing child is taken into custody by the youth authorities pending a court hearing, that the accused parent must leave the home before the child can return, and that both the parents and the child must undergo therapy with a court-appointed psychologist in order to come to grips with what has happened and why. At all times, there is concern for the child's well-being to ensure that she not be further traumatized.

However, as well-made and well-intended as *Something About Amelia* undeniably is, it lies by omission by presenting only one side of one case study, by assuming that children never lie about being molested, and by implying that the entire legal process in itself doesn't traumatize children even more than they are already. First of all, not all molestation cases are proven; at least 10 percent of accused parents aren't guilty of anything. They are the victims of children who have conjured up stories out of spite or fanciful imagination. This is clearly what happened in Scott County, Minnesota, in 1984, where an entire community was smeared by a child molestation witch hunt without foundation. In that case, 21 charges of molestation, child pornography and homicide were dropped when it turned out the children were lying about all of it, though a few other child sex abuse charges were vindicated. And one of the child witnesses in the McMartin Pre-School case in Los Angeles told a story under oath about playing a game called "Naked Movie Star," later recanting his story as a big fib. After 18 months of inconsistent and recanted testimonies by the children, and a lack of photographic evidence, charges against five of the McMartin seven were dropped by L.A. District Attorney Ira Reiner on January 17, 1986. Moreover, the alleged videotapes in the Sacramento ritual child murder case were never found, nor were any of the bodies, because it turned out the children had been lying about the whole affair. This isn't to say that all chidlren are or should be suspect, but that the margin for error in stories told by

children—many of whom are influenced by what they see on television or tell lies to please the adult investigators—is overlooked or willfully ignored in the zeal to do so-called justice.

Moreover, in order to join the therapy group known as Parents United—which Ted Danson is shown doing at the end of *Something About Amelia,* though the group isn't named—the accused parent has to admit guilt even if he or she is innocent, a fact the movie conveniently neglects to mention in favor of an upbeat ending. The reason for joining this group is that the accused parent is told it will help retrieve their children faster or will help reunite the family, which it often does not do.

Furthermore, the child often suffers from this parental separation. According to Terry Hopwood, Secretary for the Los Angeles-based Victims of Child Abuse Legislation (VOCAL), "There are many cases where the child is actually more traumatized being removed from the home than by being left in it. This occurs most frequently in cases where it turns out that no molestation actually occurred, where there's been an error of some kind. In fact, court-appointed psychologists agree this is often the case, but they are so cowed by the system they're afraid to bring it up in open court. The function of the Department of Public Social Services (DPSS) is supposedly to protect the child and keep families together; splitting up a family is only supposed to be a last resort, according to their own regulations. In practice, the first thing that happens is family separation, frequently for weeks or months until the case is resolved."

Undoubtedly, the large audience for *Something About Amelia* helped to bring out in the open a subject that badly needed clarification and public discussion, but it is also true that this movie did as much harm as good. In the bulletin for VOCAL, Arthur Tarlow, Chairman for VOCAL's Los Angeles chapter, states that "Child protection agencies across the country reported a quantum increase in such reports after the showing of [the movie]. ... It was found out later that many of their reports were not true. ... Custody battles sometimes pit the child against one of the parents and they are encouraged to lie. And, of course, sometimes the parent will lie thinking, mistakenly, that they will get the child back if they report their ex-spouse to DPSS. The children are always victims. They are victims of parental severance, humiliation, and an overloaded and often uncaring system."

As the above quotes and analyses make clear, *Something About Amelia* was only a first, though

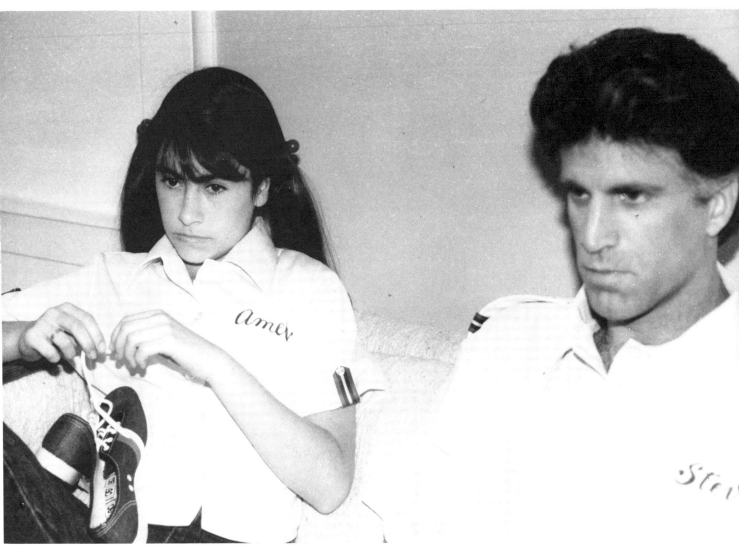

But the glum looks of Danson and Zal in this shot hint at their real, more emotionally damaging relationship of father/daughter incest. (Courtesy MGM/UA)

commendable and dramatically very good, step toward mass public education about incest and its aftermath. Where it fell short of its goal was in idealizing the legal system for child sex abuse cases when, in fact, that system is often not nearly as humane or concerned as depicted.

More movies about incest will undoubtedly be made, but whether they will be serious examinations of the problem in all its facets or titillating exploitation dramas remains to be seen. The subject has by no means been exhausted, so one can only hope that future movies dealing with it do take the sort of rational and humane approach demonstrated by *Murmur of the Heart* and *Something About Amelia*.

Cat woman Nastassia Kinski in Cat People *(1982) is stunned to learn from cat brother Malcolm McDowell that the only sex she can have is with him because of their tribal background.*

Back to the Future *(1985): Michael J. Fox meets his mother (Lea Thompson) 30 years ago. She is attracted to him, but he has to be cool toward her or he will literally cease to exist.*

Chapter 8
KINKY SEX, RAPE AND VIOLENCE

"There's a darkness inside all of us. Some act it out. Some try to control it. Most of us walk a tightrope between the two."—Janet MacLachlan in *Tightrope.*

The phrase "kinky sex" usually conjures up images of bizarre bondage and dominance games and sadomasochistic rituals, leading to bruises, permanent marks, mutilation and sometimes death. We think of sick, twisted, degenerate people who obviously hate themselves and take it out on others through kidnap, torture and murder. The history of psychopathology is loaded with case studies of individuals for whom S&M and other forms of aberrant sexual behavior are symptoms of a larger dysfunction going back to childhood. They see the darkness within and react to it by punishing others, viewing their acts as a form of love or self-righteous retribution.

That's *one* side of it.

The other side is that there are tens of thousands of outwardly normal, decent, respectable people for whom B&D and S&M—otherwise known as "the scene"—connotes control over another person as a master or loss of control to another person as a slave, relinquishing all decision-making in obedient servitude. In short, individualized fascism. Thousands of affluent professional men pay professional dominant women to help them lose control as a relief from the rigors of being dominant themselves. For thousands more, the scene is a serious, mutually consentual lifestyle in which a master or mistress controls or "owns" a male or female slave or a stable of slaves. The professed goal is not to inflict harm or damage, or to induce trauma, but to get in touch with that dark side, to control it for creatively painful pleasure, self-contradictory though that sounds.

Semi-underground clubs such as The Society of Janus in San Francisco and Los Angeles, and The Eulenspiegel Society in New York, cater to this lifestyle. Their avowed purpose is to let their own kind know they aren't alone and to enlighten curious others as to the "true" nature of the scene, which is to act out fetishes and fantasies in a controlled environment.

Dominatrix Bulle Ogier in La Maitresse *(1977) caters to a masochist who's into rubber masks…*

…then chains him up in her dungeon while commanding her "maid" to kiss her feet and do her bidding. (Courtesy Landmark Theatres)

Unfortunately, the practice of bondage and S&M is often less disciplined than the intent because people in the scene sometimes do get beaten, bruised, marked for life, sexually abused and mutilated. There are some vicious, mentally disturbed people in S&M who do not respect limitations, but it should also be noted that there are others who approach these fantasy scenes sensually, with care and compassion and the view that a top/bottom partnership is based on mutual need. For these people, many of whom are only into B&D, it is an ultimate act of love in which spankings, whippings, suspensions, piercings and other forms of dominant/submissive behavior are not only a daily reality, they are *the* reality.

Before going any further, let us separate bondage from sadomasochism by defining the parameters of each. Bondage is just what the word implies: mental and/or physical restriction with the slave being bound and sometimes gagged for servitude. Handcuffs, ropes, silk cords, chains, suspension bars and other devices are used for binding. S&M is the more extreme routine because it involves mild to extreme physical torture of all parts and organs, particularly the erogenous zones. The trick here is to inflict pain without leaving marks or drawing blood, though many masochists prefer a mark of "ownership" such as a ring through the nose, penis, vagina or nipple. Still others yearn for mutilation in the form of castration or irreparable vaginal damage, and there are some psychotic sadists willing to oblige. I will qualify that by stating that this latter group is a minority within a minority, not at all typical of the larger part of the scene.

Most of the movies dealing with this scene are underground works produced by people involved in it. These include notorious east coast personalities such as Mistress Candice and porn star Annie Sprinkle; popular west coast dominas such as Mistresses Stephanie Locke, Tantala Ray, and Lana White; a Chicago group called Intervisions, Inc., whose founder, Dave Nesor (publisher of Leather Underground), produces a variety of explicit S&M and B&D films distributed through his subsidiary company, The Mole; and a west coast firm called House of Milan, which offers relatively tamer fare. For afficionados, these hardcore productions—usually devoid of story and characterization, concentrating solely on action—are the real thing. Most of them are primitively filmed or taped, but for connoisseurs they offer undiluted voyeuristic pleasure.

Mild bondage and torture scenes are *de rigueur* in most mainstream horror and adventure movies, but in the classic genre films these are generally in the realm of playful make-believe. The mainstream seldom delves into this netherworld seriously, and when it does the results are usually softcore, rarely depicting the heavier stuff for fear of scaring off the mass audience; rarer still is any exploration of the quirks that compel these acts so that we can understand what motivates people to go kinky. Hollywood filmmakers are simply afraid to honestly, matter-of-factly explore the outer regions of the dark side for fear of tapping a collective nerve that most people would rather leave untapped.

One of the most famous movies dealing with bondage is *The Story of O* (1975), Just Jaeckin's (pronounced Jahkeen) adaptation of the European bestseller by Pauline Reage. Reage struck a chord with millions of readers with the notion that most women secretly yearn to be subjugated by men and fantasize being indoctrinated into a life of unquestioning servitude to them. (Dominant women, of course, take the opposite view.) In this adaptation, a woman known only as O (Corinne Clery) is taken by her lover (Udo Kier) to a dungeon chalet in France called The Chateau, where she is put through this indoctrination, with no explanation given as to why she lets herself in for this ordeal, though we infer that the idea of it turns her on.

Later, O's "ownership" is transferred to her lover's best friend, middle-aged master Anthony Steel. Steel's graying, bearded visage is meant to signify maturity, but you have to ask yourself how mature or secure or manly any man is who feels compelled to abuse a woman as his sexual inferior. Furthermore, he is just as dependent upon her as she is upon him because, without her, he has no one with whom to play his manipulative games.

The importance of *The Story of O* lies not in its meager, tedious "drama" but in its single-minded concern with a brutalistic fantasy world not often explored by regular movies. It provides followers of the scene with a dramatization of what drew them to it in the first place, while leaving outsiders mystified because the psychology of control is side-stepped. The movie is all effect and no cause, though the effects obviously offer vicarious satisfaction to armchair sadists and masochists.

Another cult movie, this time in the S&M genre, is *La Maitresse* (1978), which is far more graphic in its tortures, with men this time on the receiving end of the whips and chains. Bulle Ogier is head mistress here, striking up a kinky romance with sneak thief Gerard Depardieu in her swanky dungeon. There is a lot of psychopathology here, but if there is a message behind it, that message is obliterated by an endless dwelling on the sick fantasies of men who should be in therapy. The "highlight" is an excruciating scene in which a real-life dominatrix actually nails a man's penis to a board, drawing blood.

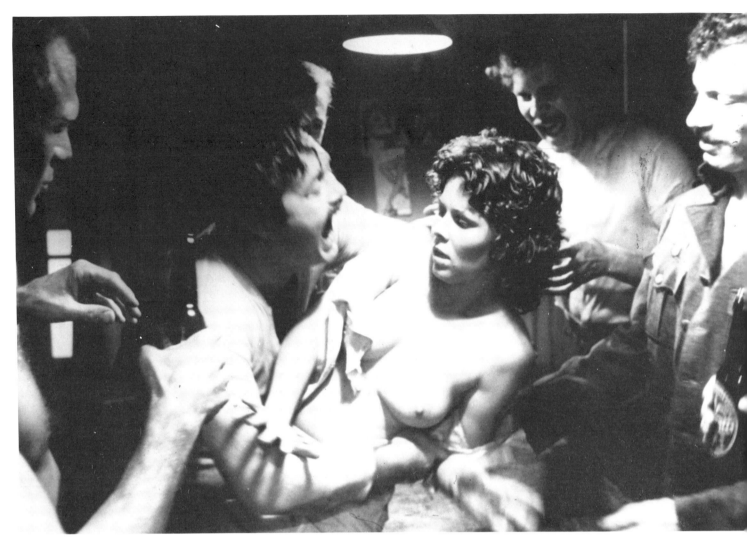

Off-duty Nazi officers pass around a lovely young prisoner in Ilsa, She Wolf of the SS *(1975).*

Nazi mythology is also a solid basis for a B&D/S&M epic, considering all the torture stories that are part of that mythology. For decades, movies have shown us that Nazi officers were all innate sadists, eager to use their Jewish prisoners for all kinds of lethal experiments.

There is as much horrific truth in these tales as there is pulp fiction—especially from the career of Josef Mengele, who never received the punishment he deserved—making them grist for movies like *Ilsa, She Wolf of the SS* (1975) and *Madam Kitty* (or *Salon Kitty,* 1976). *Ilsa* ghoulishly exploits sick preoccupations with concentration camp "experiments," while *Madam Kitty* caters to the fetish crowd with its "historical" depiction of a World War II German whorehouse where the whores cater to kinky Nazi officers. (Are there any other kind?) Neither movie provides any real insight to their depraved milieus, but at least they don't pretend to be anything more than exploitational grindhouse junk.

Mary Woronov in Eating Raoul *(1982) is dressed as Minnie Mouse to lure a kinky client so that hubby Paul Bartel (left) can bop him to death with a frying pan, take his money and dispose of him. (Courtesy Landmark Theatres)*

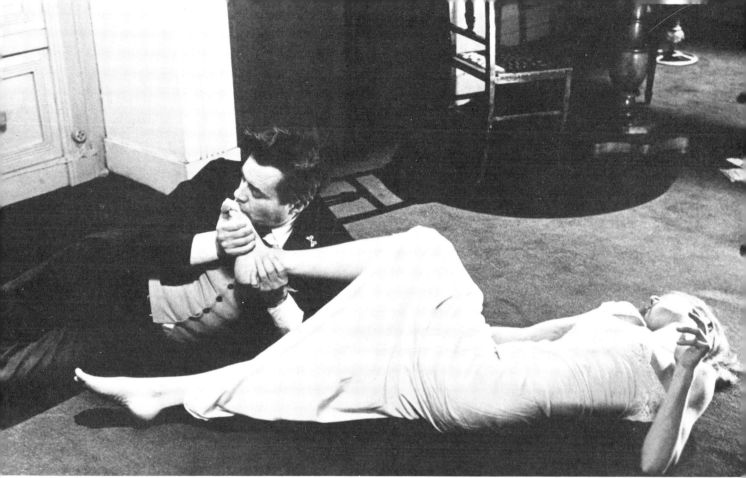

When he isn't knocking her around in true Nazi fashion, Dirk Bogarde loves to smooch Charlotte Rampling's toes in The Night Porter *(1974).*

Phony preacher Tony Perkins in Crimes of Passion *(1984) seems to be offended by hooker Kathleen Turner's toes.*

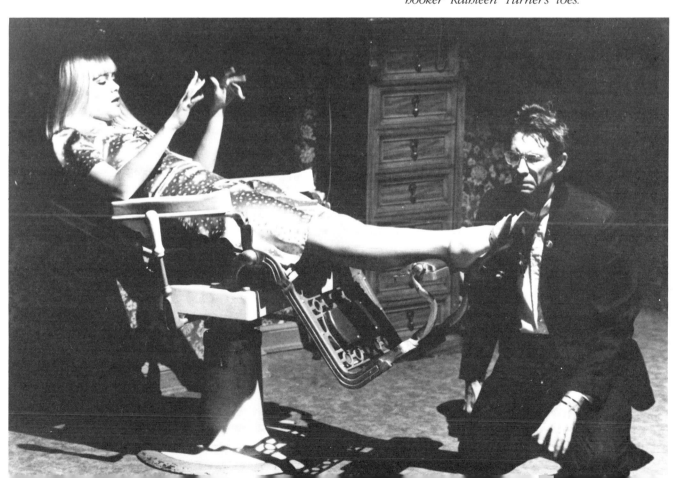

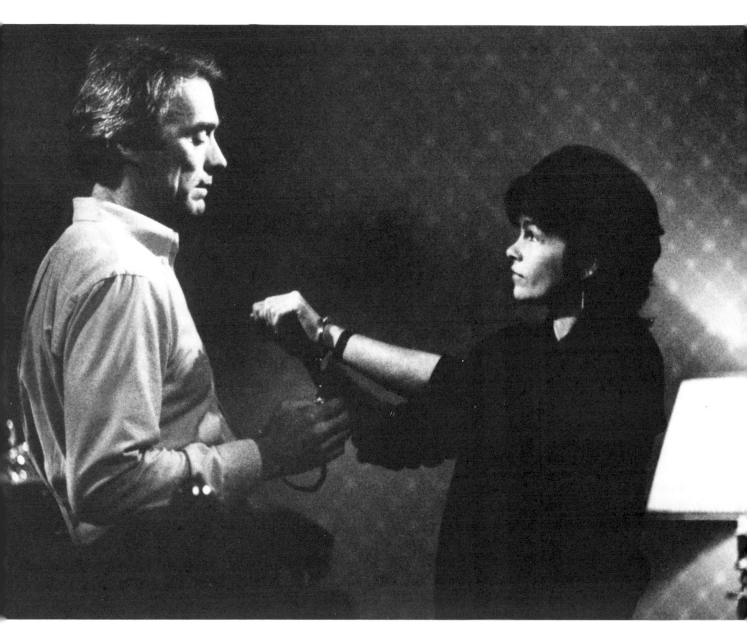

Homicide cop Clint Eastwood is tempted to do more with those handcuffs than just give social worker Genevieve Bujold a demonstration of their practical use in Tightrope *(1984).*

The same cannot be said of *The Night Porter* (1973), which tries to parlay a somber mood into an impression of an "art" film. This movie not only explores the perverse relationship between an ex-Nazi "doctor" (Dirk Bogarde) and his favorite former victim (Charlotte Rampling), it wallows in it, glorifying Nazism in the process. There are numerous concentration camp flashbacks and several present-day scenes showing former SS officers relieving their guilt for the holocaust through pseudo group therapy sessions, but there is little bondage or S&M for the devoted buffs for whom this movie was presumably intended. What we get for the most part is a tedious, moody character study of two depraved adults who aren't worth the celluloid.

The most famous B&D/S&M movie of the 80's is Robert Van Ackeren's hugely popular *A Woman in Flames* (1983, q.v. also chapter on Prostitutes), in which a contemporary German whore (Gudrun Land-grebe) turns dominatrix in contempt for the middle-class clientele she serves. She too has a dark side, turning it to her financial advantage by giving submissive men—affluent professionals with deep-seated kinks—their money's worth of whippings, leather bindings and haughty verbal abuse. The more she punishes them, the more they tip her; the more she whips them, the more she takes pleasure in it. Her live-in lover/business partner, a male prostitute (Mathieu Carriere), is disgusted when he discovers what she is doing upstairs in their apartment, fearing he too might become her slave because he cannot relate at all to the mentality of bondage. B&D buffs will certainly relate to the bondage scenes, which are spare and brief, but for others they are lacking in explanation and insight: why it is that Landgrebe revels in being dominant and what it is that compels these men to pay her to control them, to crush them literally under her heels, making them feel puny and worthless, and loving every agonizing minute of it.

The most important *American* film in years dealing with kinky sex is *Tightrope* (1984). Important because it stars Clint Eastwood, a major macho actor. Eastwood plays a New Orleans cop who is divorced and gets his kicks playing bondage games with whores. He is also being stalked by a psychopathic ex-cop bent on killing these whores. The not-so-subtle thematic point is that the killer is Eastwood's doppelganger, his sadistic side gone murderous. Though Richard Tuggle's script and direction mildly subvert Eastwood's macho cop persona by showing that persona's darker side, they are a cheat in that they resolutely refuse to make a committed plunge into the core of this seamy underworld so that not only do we see what goes on inside in a realistic rather than exploitative manner—we get only the barest hints of Eastwood's games—but gain some glimmer of understanding as to why it is there and why Eastwood in particular is drawn to it. The only insight we are allowed is when Eastwood is asked why he is divorced. He says that "I tried to show some tenderness, but it turned out she didn't want any." Does this mean his wife enjoyed being handcuffed to the bed? If so, why did they separate, since he was willing to oblige? Or can he only do it with whores? No explanation is given.

In short, almost every major American and foreign film that draws on bondage and sadomasochism for its drama either approaches the subject with a timidity verging on embarrassment, or else gets so caught up in kinky sex for its own sake that all these unexplained, motiveless acts can't help looking abnormal or sick because there is no underlying psychology, only a pretense at it, *if* we're lucky. None of this matters commercially because every movie I've discussed either has a cult following or, like *Tightrope,* is a huge financial success—especially on home video—because it does have a major star playing an unexpected turn on his accustomed image. Moviegoers are obviously content to pay for all of this decadent titillation without substance, and therefore to gain no understanding of what it is in them and others that is gratified by these movies. At least the underground films have nothing for which to apologize, because they deliver the goods they promise to their specialized audience, with no pretense at even a modicum of pop psychology.

Believe it or not, hooker Season Hubley in Vice Squad *(1982) is dressed in wedding attire for an eccentric old trick who loves to play corpse and bride.*

Kathleen Turner
in Crimes of Passion *will
play out any fantasy, no
matter how weird. Here
she is a Miss Liberty for an
obviously worshipful cli-
ent.*

Mariana Hill (left) and Donna Wilkes are group therapy patients who end up bound and gagged by a mad killer in Schizoid *(1980). (Courtesy William Margold)*

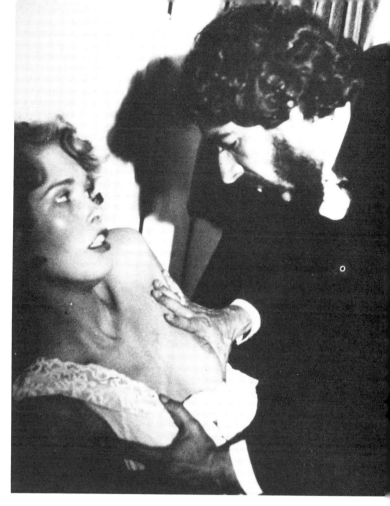

Bearded Dracula Jamie Gillis hungrily eyes Serena's exposed breast in Dracula Sucks *(1979). (Courtesy William Margold)*

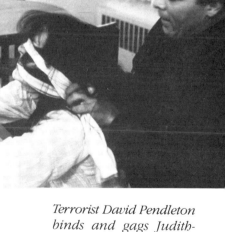

Psychotic killer Kip Niven is determined to have his way with disc jockey Roz Kelley in New Year's Evil *(1981). (Courtesy William Margold)*

Terrorist David Pendleton binds and gags Judith-Marie Bergan prior to raping her in The Abduction *(1975). The movie is about a Patty Hearst-like coed kidnapped by leftists. (Courtesy William Margold)*

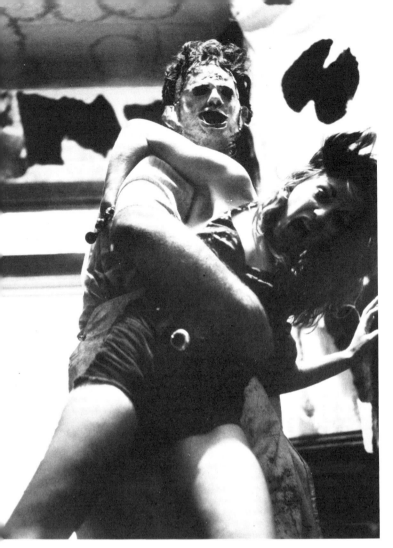

In The Texas Chain Saw Massacre *(1974), a terrified young woman is led to the slaughter by a crudely masked psychopath. (Courtesy William Margold)*

Violence is also a form of sexual perversity in the movies, and Lord knows it is prevalent in today's cinema in heavy doses as a substitute for genuine sexual feeling. The huge number of stalk-and-slash horror movies made since 1979, typified by the *Friday the 13th* series and the *Halloween* sequels, are a perfect example of commercial mayhem. Almost all of these movies cash in on the Oedipus complex or the male fear of sexually aggressive women by catering to the male audience's yearning for vicarious revenge on mommies or independent-minded women who they feel have symbolically castrated them. Movie producers have been delighted to sate this sick need with a passion, conjuring a variety of horrific means for graphically dismembering women with ghoulish, gory glee. A few of these movies, such as *Sweet Sixteen* (1982), have shown the women getting revenge on the men for real or imagined crimes, but mainly it is the men who are getting their psychotic thrills. The majority of these movies, either way, are unmitigated trash that could easily be incinerated with no apology to cinematic posterity.

In one of the few graphically horrific moments in the fine horror film, Halloween *(1978), a mad killer Kyle Richards strangles sexy P.J. Soles with a telephone cord.*

Barbara Bouchet in The Black Belly of the Tarantula *(1972) is knifed to death by her socialite husband. (Courtesy William Margold)*

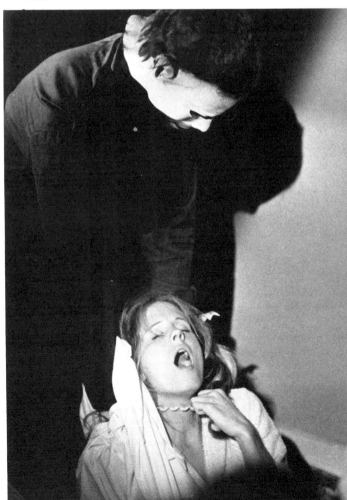

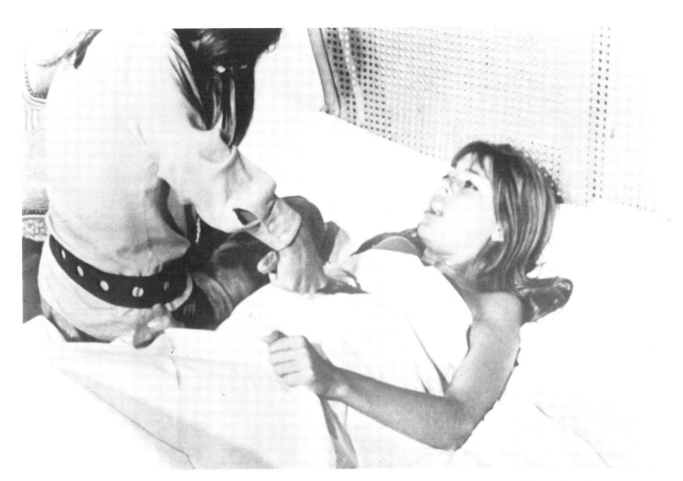

Snuff *(1975) was an Argentine import purporting to deliver the ultimate in sexual sadism. (Courtesy of William Margold)*

Countless Halloween *ripoffs have simply terrorized and slashed without the cinematic style or flair of the original. In* Friday the 13th Part III *in 3D (1982), psycho killer Richard Vrooker attempts to strangle Dana Kimmel.*

In Sam Peckinpah's supremely violent commentary on macho manhood, Straw Dogs *(1971), a village goon grabs Susan George for a gang rape while hubby Dustin Hoffman is off duck hunting.*

In Stanley Kubrick's A Clockwork Orange *(1971), Malcolm McDowell sardonically assaults Adrienne Corri using both his phallic nose and a porcelain dildo.*

Rape is also a kinky staple: to incite vigilante outrage, to exploit a female star, or to confirm the deranged notion that most women really do enjoy sexual violation. The latter is graphically demonstrated in Sam Peckinpah's *Straw Dogs* (1971), in which libidinous Susan George seemingly gets what's coming to her from a bunch of macho thugs, eventually accepting and enjoying what's being done to her, while the film cross-cuts to a scene of her seemingly ineffectual husband, Dustin Hoffman, duck hunting. We're supposed to think he's insensitive or that he condones the rape, but unless he is psychic how is he supposed to know what's going on back home?

Rape as outrage was perpetrated with satiric intent in Stanley Kubrick's *A Clockwork Orange* (1971), and to incite audience bloodlust in Clint Eastwood's *Sudden Impact* (1984). While both movies pretended to a noble social purpose in depicting their various rapes, the actual effect in both cases was to titillate while engendering a murderous desire for revenge. Malcolm McDowell in Kubrick's movie was brainwashed into goodness so that we'd feel sorry for him when he is pummeled by his former victims and angry at the social hypocrisy that robbed him of his freedom of choice to do good or evil, while macho cop Eastwood aids Sondra Locke in wasting the gang of thugs who raped her and her sister to make us feel that justice was done. These directors differed in their avowed motivations for dramatizing rape—Kubrick's was sardonic social commentary while Eastwood's was vicarious riddance of the scum of the earth—but neither director seemed especially concerned with the real-life trauma and social repercussions of rape except as it furthered the pandering commercial potential of their movies.

Rape as exploitation occurred in *Lipstick* (1976) and *The Seduction* (1982). *Lipstick* tried to have it both ways by encouraging us to join in the fun of Margaux Hemingway's being beaten, tied down and anally violated by Chris Sarandon, then reproaching us for this "pleasure" by making a social statement about the horror of rape. *The Seduction* had Andrew Stevens violating newscaster Morgan Fairchild's privacy, first as a peeping tom, then by barging into her living room to snap photos against her will, finally by vowing to cut her throat if she doesn't let him have her. Both movies are so obviously hypocritical—again we are meant to be aroused while being enraged—that you have to wonder why Hemingway and Fairchild agreed to make them.

The most exploitative of all directors when it comes to violating women is Brian DePalma with his psychopathic duo *Dressed to Kill* (1980) and *Body Double* (1984), both Hitchcock rip-offs. In these movies, mature, sexy women are tools to involve us in

When sultry TV newswoman Morgan Fairchild is assaulted by peeping tom Andrew Stevens in The Seduction *(1982), the message is clearly that she brought it on herself with her seductive TV image.*

Larry Daniels strangles his latest victim after raping her in The Rape Killer *(1976). (Courtesy William Margold)*

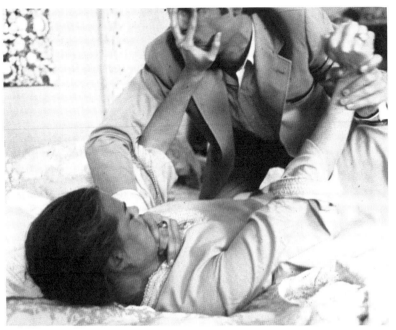

the chase for a deranged killer, who is clearly the director's misogynist alter ego.

In *Dressed to Kill,* Angie Dickinson fantasizes being raped in her shower (the body isn't hers but that of a professional model), later enjoying a real "zipless fuck" with a stranger she meets at a museum. To punish her for these imagined and real adulteries, DePalma has her slashed to death by a mad killer *after* the act of illicit sex, thereby announcing that she deserves what she gets for being such a faithless slut. When the killer goes after other women, all of them prostitutes, DePalma's theme is clear: women are a pack of whores deserving to be killed.

Model Mariel Hemingway faced the same media image dilemma in the equally re-pugnant Lipstick *(1976), here trying to fight off pervert Chris Sarandon.*

(Below) Angie Dickinson fantasizes being raped in her shower in Dressed to Kill *(1980)...*

Body Double—a rip-off of *Rear Window* and *Vertigo*—continues this misogyny by having another woman (Deborah Shelton) graphically murdered, this time with a huge, phallic chain drill that literally rips her guts out. This time, the woman is murdered because her husband (Gregg Henry) wants to collect her insurance. It's a valid plot line, but because the murder is so gruesome—it could just as easily have been done with a knife or a gun—it comes off as an excuse for DePalma to vent his anti-female hostility.

Most critics either lap at DePalma's obeisance to Hitchcock or condemn it as style without substance. What they fail to condemn is what really matters: the use of stylistics to victimize audiences with images of gore and outright hatred of women. There is nothing meritorious or praiseworthy in these movies regardless of technique, so more "substance" would be worse, not better.

Craig Wasson shares a lustful moment with Deborah Shelton in Body Double *(1984)…*

…then learns that porn actress Melanie Griffiths is really the woman he's been peering at through a telescope as part of a murderous con game in which he is the prize patsy.

Alfred Hitchcock less satirically made the audience helpless spectators to deadly assault in his hotly controversial Frenzy *(1972). Here, Barry Foster rapes Barbara Leigh-Hunt…*

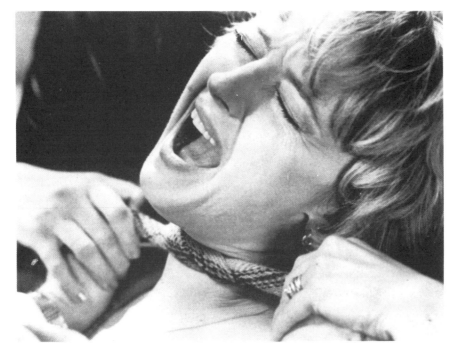

…then achieves his second climax by strangling her with his necktie. (Courtesy William Margold)

Julie Christie in Demon Seed *(1971) found herself in the clutch of a computer programmed by mad scientist hubby Fritz Weaver to impregnate her. (Courtesy William Margold)*

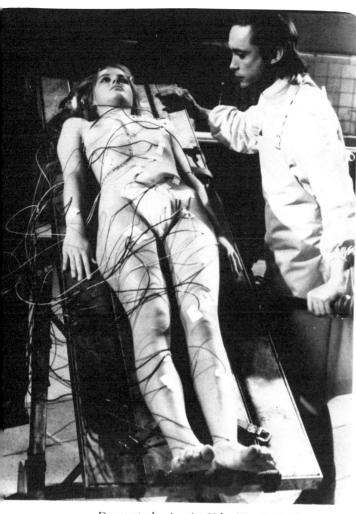

Demented scientist Udo Kier in Andy Warhol's Frankenstein *(1974) pieced together his ideal synthetic woman for acts of lustful depravity.*

This young woman is a victim of the Spanish Inquisition in the heavy-handed historical opus The Holy Office (El Santo Oficio, 1974). *(Courtesy William Margold)*

Men could be assaulted too. Teda Bracchi (far upper right) led her sister chain-gang prisoners in a gang-rape of a gay prison guard in The Big Bird Cage *(1972).*

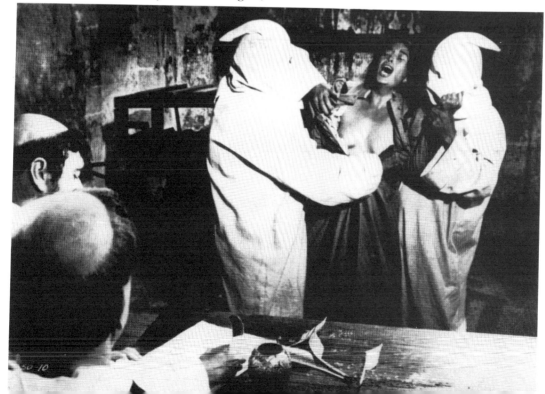

This sensual-looking warmup with Mickey Roarke and Kim Basinger in 9½ Weeks (1986) is just about as daring as this overhyped ode to S&M romance got because its dramatic guts, if any, were disemboweled in the cutting room.

Furthermore, with the release of *Scarface* (1983), DePalma finally showed his true colors by doing the one thing he loves best: murdering as many people as he can as fast as he can for as many hours as he can for sheer sadistic thrills.

The worst thing about *all* of the movies discussed and depicted in this chapter—with the notable exception of the stylishly frightening *Halloween*—is not that they pander to our basest drives and desires, but that they contribute nothing to our understanding of them, to our control of the dark side of human nature. They dwell mainly on what is meanest in us, encouraging acts of violence. By paying to see these kinds of movies over and over, we are clearly voting against our humanity in favor of misrepresentation through brutality and bloodshed, in favor of vicious men and women who will bequeath this foul legacy to their children. We are replacing the penis with phallic weapons and the vagina with bullet holes, saying that sadism is love, that death is orgasm. If life imitates art with an increasing crime rate, with growing numbers of husband and wife beaters and child molesters, influenced in part by these movies, who do we really have to blame?

Or do we care?

Chapter 9
HARDCORE PORNOGRAPHY

"Nixon's administration did a study on porn proving that the *absence* of it led to sex crimes. Of course, they never let the American people know the results. Denmark has legalized prostitution, with no report of a single rape for five years. I wish that Women Against Porn would listen to the facts!"—Porn star Hyapatia Lee

"No one ever died from an overdose of pornography."—Porn star William Margold

When *A Pictorial History of Sex in Films* was published, hardcore pornography had just gotten underway as a socially chic and acceptable evening at the movies. The stereotype of dirty old businessmen in raincoats gave way to images of dating and married couples taking in cause célèbres such as *Deep Throat, The Devil in Miss Jones* and *Behind the Green Door,* all released in 1972.

Linda Lovelace became the nation's porno darling in *Deep Throat* by parlaying a gimmick—fellatio down to the base of the penis—into one-picture stardom, later denying she had enjoyed any of it in her book *Ordeal.* Georgina Spelvin became the first plain-looking female porn star as a spinster suicide who insists on sexual purgatory in *The Devil in Miss Jones.* If she is going to hell for having killed herself, at least she is going to have done something to deserve such a fate. And Marilyn Chambers shocked the nation in *Behind the Green Door* because here was literally the

girl next door—the mother on the Ivory Soap box—being coerced into taking part in a live nightclub sex show, with super-endowed black stud Johnny Keyes as one of the performers.

None of these films on their own terms have any artistic merit. Once you get past the gimmick of a woman having her clitoris in her throat, *Deep Throat* becomes a wretched bore at little more than an hour in length. *The Devil in Miss Jones*—produced and directed by Gerard Damiano, who also made *Deep Throat*—has above-average production values, but the sex is far from erotic, particularly when Spelvin makes love to a snake and to another woman while both of them are covered in oil. And *Behind the Green Door,* while it does boast Marilyn Chambers' erotic presence (when she finally got to talk in *The Resurrection of Eve,* she proved she couldn't act), is also pretty dull, especially its celebrated multi-exposure, slow-motion cum shot. The best thing about the first two movies is

Analyzing Linda Lovelace's problems in Deep
Throat *(1972).*

132

Harry Reems, whose genuine comic and dramatic talents are wasted.

The best that can be said about any of these movies is that they brought cinematic pornography out of the closet into the mainstream of moviegoing, converting a large underground operation with a hugely profitable male following into a major film industry. Moreover, hardcore pornography has created its own star system, acted as the catalyst for and savior of dozens of boringly identical sex magazines, and reaped hundreds of millions of dollars in home video sales and rentals, cornering nearly a third of the home video market in the United States.

Because it *is* so open and prolific, pornography has been denounced by legal and religious watchdogs as obscene, filthy, degenerate and corruptive of teen-age and adult morals. The more popular the stuff becomes, the more groups like Jerry Falwell's Liberty Foundation and activists like Andrea Dworkin seek to suppress it (mainly to make names for themselves), thereby making it even more attractive. What is tagged as taboo or dirty always has the allure of forbidden fruit. Softcore director Russ Meyer set out to dramatize this in his only straight dramatic movie, *The Seven Minutes* (1971), made before pornography became big box-office. Though seriously intended, the movie is ludicrous because Meyer plays it for winks and leers.

All of which begs the questions of what exactly is pornography and whether or not viewing it can be healthy or harmful. First of all, let us define the term pornography, which is easy enough to do: It is the literal, graphically explicit, verbal or visual depiction of sexual intercourse, be it vaginal, oral or anal. In short, the actual depiction of people engaged in sex. Softcore porn differs from the hard version in that the acts are implied or shown, but actual penetration or oral stimulation is not shown.

As for its socially redeeming value, the truth is that most pornography is not obscene or filthy or most of those other pejoratives. What it is for the most part is formulaic and boringly repetitive. Most porno films consist of a plot device as an excuse for long and barely edited sequences of men and women—straight, bisexual and homosexual—pumping in and out of each other with as much feeling as a jackhammer. Precious little of it is erotic; most of it is merely vicarious wish fulfillment. In most porno movies you can count on: missionary scenes, woman-on-top scenes, endless oral sex scenes, a rape scene, a lesbian scene, a woman orally stimulating two or more men or vice-versa, and group sex.

With few exceptions, you could take the standard hardcore scenes from any ten porno features, mix

Miss Lovelace in a contemplative mood.

Marilyn Chambers and that famous Ivory Snow box.

A Roman orgy in progress. One of the few mild scenes from the quasi-pornographic Caligula *(1979). (Courtesy Landmark Theatres)*

them up, put them back in different films, and you wouldn't know the difference because, even though some of the faces change, the same stars appear with monotonous regularity doing the same old things to each other. The titles change and the plot devices vary, but the people who make these movies have boxed the genre into a self-limiting, thunderously oppressive set of clichés and banalities. Most of them haven't awakened to the fact that their audience has changed and demands better, more sophisticated, more compassionate material.

In that sense, pornography *is* corrupting because if you watch enough of it, you get a twisted sense of what lovemaking is all about: rutting bodies going through all sorts of gyrations and routines without joy or friendliness or a sense of intimacy. It is mainly a lot of depersonalized sex, much of which caters to male fantasies of being orally gratified by women, and once one has masturbated to climax over one of these acts, the remaining half dozen are very dull indeed if there isn't a good story with believable characters to hold one's interest.

George C. Scott is unbelievably distraught upon seeing his teenage daughter in a porno film. It was her *choice after all. From* Hardcore *(1978).*

Pornography *is* healthy to the extent that it vicariously fulfills a variety of fantasies—men identify with the well-endowed studs having sex with all the beautiful women, and women dream about the studs because of their looks, size, prowess and stamina; that it's cheaper than going to prostitutes; that it's an outlet for aggression; and that it provides a stimulus for lovers, bored couples and swing singular parties. Seen in *that* light, it's a marvelous safety valve and inspiration, but too much of it as a steady diet can result in a sordid and cynical outlook on real romance where sex is an expression of love and sharing, not just the end product of unthinking lust. And, if you're a film buff, a glut of porn can give you a healthier respect for mainstream movies with good production values, solid storylines and complex characters.

Another myth about porn is that women are abducted to star in these films and are forced to perform the acts or be sexually abused and sometimes murdered, as in the snuff films hoax of the mid-70's. Director Paul Schrader set out to prove these notions in *Hardcore* (1979), in which Calvinist midwesterner George C. Scott trails his missing daughter (Ilah Davis) to Hollywood, where he finds himself caught in a web of unspeakable perversions and depravity. In point of fact, nothing could be further from the truth and Schrader knows it; he claimed or admitted in more than one interview that not only did he do no research prior to writing and directing *Hardcore,* but that he turned down offers of technical advice from the porno industry.

Porno actor/writer/director William Margold refutes Schrader's statements, saying, "I was hired for $200 to bring in porn star Serena and to arrange the filming of the loop featuring Ilah Davis." Margold also knows the abduction theory of *Hardcore* is bogus because he used to cast almost half the movies that were made in 1973-82 and he always made a point of warning the women—and men—of what they were getting into in terms of sex and image. Neither he nor any other casting agent or producer forces anyone to make these movies, let alone murders them. Yes, there is drug taking and kinky sex among porn people, but the same can be said of mainstream Hollywood, only more so, so who is kidding whom?

A final myth is that porn producers molest children by seducing or abducting them into porn. There is no truth in this. There *are* kiddie porn films and there *is* an underground American market for them among degenerate adults, but they are not part of the above-ground porn industry nor will they ever be. *No* reputable porn filmmakers even dabble in the stuff. It is illegal, and both the Adult Film Association of America and the X-Rated Critics Organization are morally opposed to it.

What keeps the porn industry going despite the fact that 99 percent of what it churns out is predictable, horribly acted trash is an insatiable public appetite for raunchy fornication. What also keeps the industry going is its star system, which is attuned to vigorous self-promotion. Most female porn stars and some male ones do road show acts at nightclubs, strip joints and porn theatres; all of them are interviewed by the sex magazines as a matter of course, keeping their mystiques going even if they have nothing interesting to say, which they usually don't; some have fan clubs, selling tons of "personalized" merchandise by mail order; some work for the Personal Services phone sex service in Marina Del Rey; and some are courted secretly by politicians, businessmen and mainstream celebrities. All of this adds up to a potent layer of erotic glamour.

The biggest star porno has ever known, the industry's one worldwide standard, is John Holmes, who is renowned *solely* for having a 12½- to 14-inch erection, depending on where you measure from and who is doing the measuring. Holmes has made over 2500 porno shorts and features—including some gay ones—and has made love to 14,000 women on and offscreen by his own count. In private life, he is a notorious gigolo, sought after and richly paid by well-known and/or affluent women the world over *only* because he is hung like a horse. Otherwise, he is a homely-looking man with a scrawny physique and a barely above-average mentality who generally makes love onscreen with indifference. If he weren't so well-endowed, he would be a truck driver or construction worker.

Holmes came to prominence in the late 1960's through a series of cheaply made loops, becoming a star in a series of violent porno detective films in the early 70's in which he played Johnny Wadd, private dick, fast on the trigger, both metallic and sexual. Holmes couldn't act worth a damn but in movies like *Blonde Fire* (1978), his penis spoke for him, making him a sexual living legend. A few years ago, he became even more notorious when he was indicted as an accomplice in the July, 1981, Laurel Canyon murders, eventually being acquitted for lack of evidence. Because of that trial, his mystique grew and he was more in demand than ever, though porno producers had long been shopping for a better-looking actor to equal or top Holmes in size and stamina.

Porn producer Hank Berger appeared to have found Holmes's successor in 1985 when he discovered and signed a darkly good-looking young man from West Virginia whom he dubbed Dick Rambone. Rambone's size is touted as being 15½ inches, though the exact size varies depending on which sex magazine you're reading. Rambone's debut feature was a shoddy

Marilyn Chambers gets an unusual pool lesson from David Morris in Insatiable *(1980), (Courtesy William Margold)*

video quickie titled *Rambone the Destroyer* (1986), a porn takeoff on *Rambo*. Though it's supposed to showcase Rambone's sexual claim to fame, it's hard to tell if he lives up to his billing due to a lack of close-ups and inept camera work in general. Does Rambone out-inch Holmes or is he merely quite large for his height and build? Perhaps his latest movies in 1986, *Rambone Does Hollywood* and *Rambone Meets the Double Penetrators,* will show us for sure (if anybody cares), but even if they do make him popular with

porn watchers—especially women—it is doubtful that he will succeed Holmes as the King of Porn or even become an enduring genre star because he has no personality or screen presence.

The opposite of Holmes in looks *and* talent is Veronica Hart, undoubtedly the best actress ever to appear in porno films. Most of the best movies in the genre have in common the fact that she is the star. What is unique about Hart (who has appeared on talk shows like Phil Donahue's) is not just that she is

Clockwise from the top: Samantha Fox, Veronica Hart, and Kelly Nichols.

gorgeous and has screen presence, but that she is a gifted, classically trained actress with a wide range who has singlehandedly imbued the genre with the sense of humanity it was sorely lacking.

She was only in the business for a few years and a few dozen movies, retiring in 1982 to sell erotic mail-order goodies and pursue a mainstream film career which so far has eluded her, but for the brief time she was part of it, she made porno movies an event. In

Eric Edwards and Jessie St. James touch lips tenderly while showering in Charli *(1981).*

films like *Games Women Play, Amanda By Night, Indecent Exposure, The Playgirl, Wanda Whips Wall Street,* and *Roommates,* she was the porn equivalent of Jean Arthur and Carole Lombard: charming, romantic, bawdy, lascivious, sensuous and vulnerable. When she is performing sex on screen, she looks like she is really making love, not just going through the motions. Watching her in any of these movies makes you wonder why she got into the business in the first place, why such an obviously talented woman wasn't taking her rightful place alongside Jane Fonda, Sally Field, Debra Winger and Karen Allen.

Of the movies mentioned above, the two best are *Amanda by Night* (1981) and *Roommates,* (1982). In the first, she is a hooker who splits from her pimp (Jamie Louis) to operate on her own. And what a hooker she is, a pro who cares as much about clients as she does about the money she earns. In one sequence, she gives a lesson in love to a nervous young man: she is tender, sensual, soothing and encouraging, the very essence of erotic femininity. This sequence is cross-cut with another in which hookers Samantha Fox and Lisa DeLeeuw play B&D games with a masochistic client. The contrast is a revelation for what it demonstrates about the essential difference between joyful normal sex and harsh bondage and humiliation sex. The former looks far more appealing than the latter.

In *Roommates,* Hart is an aspiring stage actress in New York. In pursuit of a career, she befriends a fellow actor (Jerry Butler) who claims to be gay, but who ends up making sweet love to her in an artfully lit, photographed and edited sequence. Again, Hart is a study in emotional range: exhilaration, camaraderie, disgust, horror, concern. *Roommates* has fewer sex scenes than most other porn movies, but what scenes there are, especially with Hart, for the most part complement the story without interrupting it; and even without them, *Roommates* is a fairly good piece of work overall.

In short, *Amanda by Night, Roommates* and the other films mentioned make a persuasive case for Hollywood producers to break a long-standing taboo against using porn actors by making Hart a legit movie star.

Hart's successor in erotic presence and acting range was voluptuous, red-haired Colleen Brennan, who has been ubiquitous in porn movies since 1983. Brennan had begun her screen career years earlier in sexploitation films using the name Sharon Kelley (she jokingly claims she is "the smallest-titted woman ever to appear in a Russ Meyer movie"), then became a phone sex operator, the most successful in America, which she still is. She later returned to acting with bit

John Leslie lets his guard down for some tender words with Raven Turner in Nothing to Hide *(1981). (Courtesy William Margold)*

Colleen Brennan.

Harry Reems.

roles in TV series like *Mannix* and *Lou Grant* before making the move to hardcore films. What is special about her is that she exudes sexuality and wanton, sluttish appeal while retaining a core of compassionate humanity, just as Hart did. Brennan revels in sex and can arouse just by standing still and smiling her playful tigress smile. Her films include *Trinity Brown, Tower of Power, Matinee Idol, 69 Park Avenue* and *Good Girl, Bad Girl,* movies that range in quality from good to fair, but which undeniably shine when she is on screen.

The roll of other first-rate porn actors is small but choice. My personal Porn Hall of Fame in alphabetical order is as follows:

—R. Bolla, a natural actor with a sardonic, often droll sense of humor in movies like *Amanda by Night* and *Centerfold Fever.* He is usually bearded but I prefer him clean-shaven.

—Rene Bond, the Princess of Porn. Petite, cute, a bundle of dynamic sexual energy in a small but irresistibly vivacious package. Her last movie was *Creme Rinse* in 1976 with John Holmes. She is gone but hardly forgotten.

—Eric Edwards, the Tyrone Power of porn in movies like *Games Women Play* and *Great Sexpectations.* An all-around actor who is smooth, handsome and charming.

—Jamie Gillis, the Marlon Brando of porn for his electric presence and versatility. He ranges from easy-going charm in *The Opening of Misty Beethoven* to his more established persona of kinky, menacing lust in movies like *Roommates.*

—Ron Jeremy, the charming, moustachioed court jester of porn who can also be commandingly dramatic. He seems to be in half the porn flicks that get made, but that's because he works cheap. He's generally a pleasure to watch in movies like *Centerfold Fever* and *Scoundrel,* but he has fallen into a rut of gabby shtick the last few years.

—John Leslie, the seducer par excellence, famous for his arrogant persona in *Talk Dirty to Me, Nothing to Hide* and *Between Lovers,* but capable of a more sensitive side as in *Every Woman Has a Fantasy* (1984).

—Pat Manning, a mature beauty with a bold sense of humor in movies like *Amanda by Night,* and *The Young Like It Hot.* The Barbara Stanwyck of porn.

—Kevin James, a handsome, charming, all-around stud in movies like *Stiff Competition.*

—Richard Pacheco, an intelligent, pleasant-looking man who convincingly ranges from retardation in *Talk Dirty to Me* to boyish innocence in *Insatiable* to romantic intellect in *The Dancers.*

—Kay Parker, a British class act with a gorgeous face, great body and lusty, compassionate brand of

Wonder woman Ann Marie mounts mounted policeman Charles Napier in Russ Meyer's softcore comedy Super Vixens *(1975). (Courtesy Eric Hoffman)*

elegance in *Taboo* (the first incest porn film), *Sex World* and *The Young Like it Hot, The Best Little Whorehouse in Texas*. She's now retired from porn acting and is publicity director for Caballero Control Corporation, a porn video distributor. She's also producing her own movies.

—Harry Reems, a classically trained actor who first made his mark in *Deep Throat* and *The Devil in Miss Jones*. He later starred in a low-budget Canadian cop film in an attempt to go legit, but returned to porn after failing to break the Hollywood barrier. He's a good actor with a wonderful comic talent who deserves better.

Sweet-looking Angel does some playful necking with Bobby Bullock in Girls on Fire *(1984). (Courtesy VCX Video)*

—Jessie St. James, now retired. A dazzling blond beauty with a terrific body and sizzling personality who steals the show in movies like *Talk Dirty to Me, Insatiable* and *Easy.* This is a lady with a lot of heart and a lot of heat.

—Jack Wrangler, a blond stud who first made his name in gay porn. He projects a relaxed, humorous, ingratiating personality in movies like *Roommates* and *Jack 'n Jill.* He has published an autobiography and made news with his romantic involvement with singer Margaret Whiting.

Honorable mentions go to:

—Angel, the porn find of the mid-80's for her pug-nosed cheerleader beauty and ability to seem both wanton and innocent at once.

—Gina Carrera, cute and spunky and with a luscious body. She debuted in the porn boxing movie parody *Stiff Competition.* A star on the rise.

—Vanessa Del Rio, the Cuban bombshell with the newly muscular body and a renowned appetite for oral sex.

—Danielle Martin, a blond sex kitten who leaps off the screen and magazine pages with a dazzling sexual presence. My vote for the Marilyn Monroe of porn.

And then there is Seka, the biggest blond porn star of all for her looks, body, breasts, star quality, and sex goddess presence. She is more popular with men than any other porn star, though her aloofness and aura of inaccessibility leave me cold.

There are scores of other personalities, both active and retired, and listing them all would be impossible here. Suffice to say that what generally counts in porn is not so much acting ability—though that has become increasingly important—as looks, build, prowess, stamina, screen presence and, for the males, a large penis, the bigger the better.

What also counts more and more is the ability to turn in a good-looking, exceptional product despite the formula limitations imposed by distributors. A handful of producer/directors have managed to break the mold. Among them:

—Russ Meyer, the King of the Nudies, a purveyor of beautifully photographed, exceptionally produced softcore comedies that are fast, bawdy, raunchy good fun. His movies include *Up!* and *Russ Meyer's Supervixens* (both 1975). His best movie is arguably *Vixen* (1968), starring Erica Gavin.

—Gerard Damiano, who broke the field wide open with *Deep Throat* and *The Devil in Miss Jones,* and who continued to break new ground with movies like the S&M-themed *The Story of Joanna* (1975).

—Radley Metzger, a.k.a. Henry Paris, whose porn classic *The Opening of Misty Beethoven* (1975) is a fast, cute, sexy takeoff on *Pygmalion*. He also gave us the fast and clever *The Private Afternoons of Pamela Mann* (1974). His trademarks are rapid editing, a keen eye for camera placement and witty scenarios.

—Chuck Vincent, who gave us *Roommates*, *Games Women Play* and *Jack 'n Jill*, proving, along with Metzger, that porn could have narrative as well as sexual thrust.

—Richard Milner, whose brisk, bawdy, hilarious *Centerfold Fever* (1982) should have made him the Mel Brooks of the X genre. He has an eye for fast-paced action and an ear for witty dialogue, both rare commodities in porn. Despite the commercial success of *Centerfold Fever,* he hasn't been able to get backing for a follow-up.

—Gail Palmer, who at age 20 with *Hot Summer in the City* (1977) became the first well-known female porn director. Though her movies weren't much better than anyone else's, they stood out for their innocently raunchy sense of fun, particularly the *Candy* series. The lead actress, Carol Connors *(Candy Goes to Hollywood)* couldn't act worth a damn, but she had big breasts to compensate and a dumb blonde persona that turned men on.

—Henri Pachard, who broke new ground in 1985 and 1986 with his ambitious *Knots Landing*-like porn serial *Taboo American Style,* a unique attempt to tell a soap opera story through explicit sex.

—And, of course, the big porn news of 1984-86, the Dark Brothers. Their productions include *Black Throat, Between the Cheeks,* and *Let Me Tell Ya 'Bout White Chicks.* They are acclaimed for their lighting effects, use of new wave rock music and elaborately staged sex scenes that go for the groin and stay there.

Other directors who have tried to be different include:

—Suze Randall, a former *Playboy* photographer whose accent is on fast, dirty fun in movies like *Stud Hunters* (1984) and *Love Bites* (1985). Her trademarks are big-busted, beautiful nymphos and handsome, well-built studs, though she would be better off concentrating more on plot and characters than contriving scripts around body parts for their own sake.

—Richard Mahler, with his penchant for existential brooding and dark, perverse sex in *Corruption* and the pretentious *Midnight Heat,* a so-called hard-boiled gangster story. Pseudo-seriousness isn't sexy *or* entertaining.

—Rinse Dream with his cult movie *Café Flesh,* set against a post-nuclear backdrop. It's a good idea but the execution is terrible, with some of the most mechanical sex scenes ever filmed.

—And William Margold, who slapped together a piece of junk called *Lust Inferno,* (1982), thinking—

Richard Bolla and Shanna McCullough smooch matter-of-factly. (Courtesy VCX Video)

Part-Cherokee Hyapatia (pronounced High-patia) Lee. On film she has a wicked grin and manner that light up the screen. (Courtesy Hyapatia Lee)

hoping—its story of a hypocritical preacher (Margold) who inadvertently commits incest with his daughter would set the porn industry in a rage. All he did was make another boring movie. Margold fancies himself the Wild Man or Bad Boy of porn, a fearless innovator, but what that mostly amounts to is slapping and humiliating women on screen for the sheer sadistic fun of it. One of his latest roles is in a porn version of *The Wizard of Oz,* called *Chastity,* shot on tape.

At times, the porn industry seems to be on the verge of cleaning up its act by making movies that really *are* movies instead of a bunch of arbitrary sex acts with some dialogue thrown in for good measure. For the most part, though, it is sex as spectator sport, enjoyable in small doses and with the right mix of ingredients. Whether or not it will ever permanently evolve to a more sophisticated state for the major productions or revert for good to its gutter origins remains to be seen, but the real question is whether very many people outside the industry really care *what* happens to it.

What *is* certain is that there is a glut of product on the market—2000 plus titles out of more than 10,000 made—and rapid growth in home video sales and rentals, putting thousands of porn theaters out of business in the process. After all, why waste time and money going to a porn theater when you can get off on porn videos in the privacy of your home? It's a lot more convenient and comfortable and anyway, most porn movies don't lose anything on a TV screen.

In the long run the video boom is good news for distributors who are making a fortune on cassette sales, including a few lines of softcore versions of hardcore originals. However, it is bad news in the long run for porn buffs who wish the emphasis were on quality rather than on assemblyline video quantity, and that the medium would finally live up to its euphemism as adult entertainment.

Chapter 10
IT IS THE SIZE THAT COUNTS

"How big are you? ... I mean, how tall are you?"—Margot Kidder to Christopher Reeve in *Superman*.

We Americans are preoccupied with size. We always want everything around us to be bigger and better, from cars to houses to boats to sex organs. We are convinced that the sheer size of something has a direct relation to its qualitative value, especially when it comes to sex. Millions of men are obsessed with women who have huge busts even though the breast is a non-functioning mammary gland except when nurturing a newborn babe. Both men and women are concerned with penis size—men probably more than women—seeing a large erect one as a physical symbol of masculine sexual prowess.

In fact, the concept of large sex organs permeates our culture: in movies, TV shows, books, songs, paintings, sculpture, advertising and so on. The huge bosom and the big bulge or large erection provide constant attention and arousal.

We are also concerned with what we *call* our organs, judging by the sheer variety of names given to the penis and breast. Yet few people are aware that while breast is an accepted scientific term for that organ, penis is only a euphemism like all the others. In fact, there is no medical or scientific term for the male sex organ except male sex organ. Penis is Latin for "tail," and the only reason it is socially more acceptable than "cock" is because of the difference in sound. "Penis" is softer, more euphonious, while "cock" is harsher, more sexually aggressive.

Whatever we call these organs in bed or in polite society, there are lots of them in movies, or at least lots of references to them. Lord knows there have been scores of female stars who are or were renowned, in part, for having big breasts. Raquel Welch, Ann-Margret, Dolly Parton, and porn stars Seka and Candy Samples are just a few who have huge male followings because they are so wonderfully well-endowed.

The same applies to male stars, but only in porno films. John Holmes, Dick Rambone, Marc Stevens, Jack

Bette Midler in Divine Madness *(1980) jokes about dating a guy who was a 10. "Well, actually a 10½."*

(Opposite page) Francesca "Kitten" Natividad admiring her 50+ wonders of the world in Beneath the Valley of the Ultravixens *(1979).*

Wrangler, Jeff Stryker, Rick Donovan, Casey Donovan, Steve York, Michael Knight, Peter North, Johnny Hardin, Al Parker and many other hardcore performers, both straight and gay, are celebrated because they sport some of the world's largest erections, not because they can act because most of them can't. Like the women, they have huge fan followings, both male and female. This is because the men vicariously identify with the virility associated with a large penis, and because the women fantasize being made love to by a hugely-endowed man, whether or not such a man would in reality give them more pain than pleasure.

It's the breasts, though, that get spotlighted in movies, both serious and exploitation. In fact, a lot of movies have been designed primarily to show off the 40+ attributes of their female leads. These include exploitation films of the early 1970's such as *The Big Doll House* and *The Big Bird Cage* (both 1972) with Pam Grier, and teen sex comedies of the late 70's through mid-80's such as *Teen Lust* ((1978), *Lunch Wagon* (1980), *Spring Break* and *Private School* in 1983, and *Hollywood Hot Tubs* in 1984, among so many others in which young women with huge bosoms were cast mainly for that reason.

Directors Russ Meyer and Federico Fellini are obsessed with big breasts. Meyer uses only the most hugely-endowed women in all of his films, sexpots like Edy Williams, Kitten Natividad and Uschi Digard, all of whose acting talent is centered in their bust size. Meanwhile, Fellini has gone out of his way to show off grossly outsized women with watermelon-sized breasts in *Amarcord* (1974), *Casanova* (1976) and *City of Women* (1979).

However, because the penis is more functional than the breast, and because most legitimate male stars shy away from showing off theirs on camera, male organ size is only alluded to in most mainstream films. In fact, judging by the number of PG- and R-rated movies made since 1970 that are entirely about penis size or in which there are coy or clever comic scenes about or references to it, you'd think that almost every red-blooded American, or British, male was secretly measuring himself first thing every morning to make sure he's big enough.

Three comedies that are entirely about the pursuit of a large male organ are *Percy* (1971), its sequel *Percy's Progress* (a.k.a. *It's Not The Size That Counts*, 1974), and *The Statue* (1971). The *Percy* films are about a lusty young man who undergoes surgery for a new and longer phallus. In the first film he *has* to get a new penis to replace his own after it's chopped off by a falling chandelier piece. In the second, he merely wants to add a few inches more, though it's never explained why.

Percy might have been a good knockabout com-

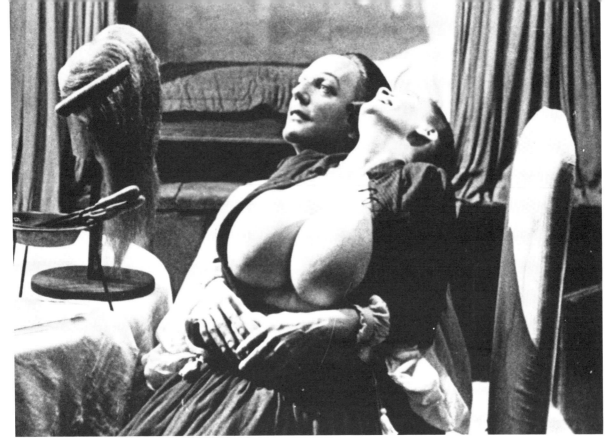

Russ Meyer, eat your heart out. Donald Sutherland as Fellini's Casanova *(1976) appears to be contemplating his good fortune in finding two of the biggest in history.*

Hywell Bennet cannot believe the size of his new organ in Percy *(1971), as Doctor Denholm Elliott proudly admires his surgical handiwork.*

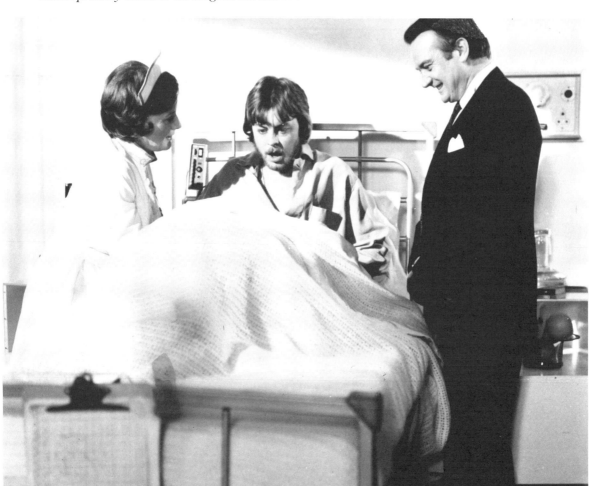

But size queen Britt Ekland is all too disbelieving because she knows she's seen that thing somewhere before.

A few years later, Percy (Leigh Lawson this time) opted for another penis transplant in It's Not the Size That Counts *(a.k.a.* Percy's Progress, 1974). *Here a British surgical team salutes him for literally rising to the occasion. Notice where the British flag is.*

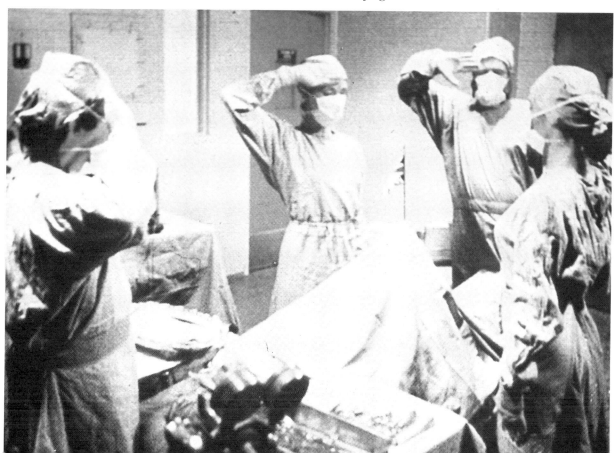

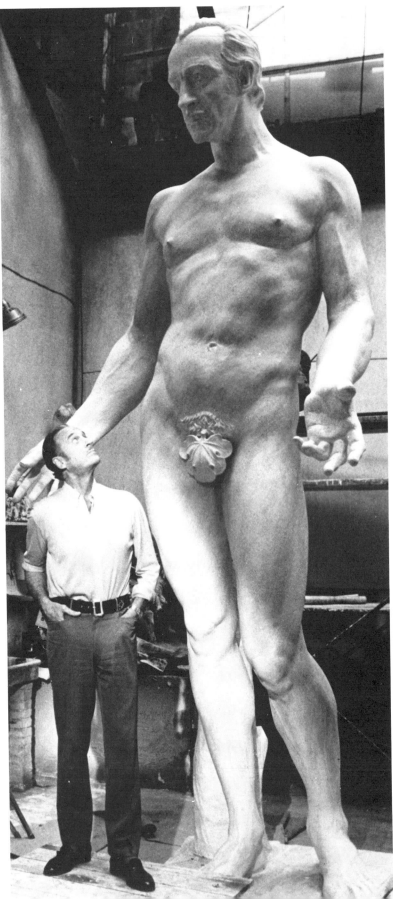

In this publicity pose for The Statue *(1971), David Niven seems to be wondering if the sculpture really does resemble him in all respects.*

edy about the various problems a young man might encounter with a larger penis than he's been used to and which doesn't do as he wants, or it could have been a comic commentary on why it is that so many women go wild over a big one. Instead of blessing his lucky size either way, Hywell Bennett as Percy spends most of the movie trying to find out who his extra millimeters came from. It turns out to have been a philandering count who has bedded the likes of Britt Ekland and Elke Sommer, obviously women of taste and discretion.

This may all sound like good, bawdy fun, but it's really no more than several reels of cheap, pandering, witless vulgarity parading as a message about the value of sensitivity versus size. Despite that, *Percy* made a lot of money, prompting a sequel in 1974 that is lots more risque fun, though a lot of critics didn't think so.

It's Not the Size that Counts (1974, a.k.a. *Percy's Progress*) is a cheerfully ribald sex farce that's as much bawdy good fun as it is embarrassing. This time, Percy (Leigh Lawson) undergoes surgery to become even better endowed. When he emerges with an erection to rival even a porn star's, he becomes the most sought-after man in England, especially by married women. Through a bizarre set of circumstances, he becomes the only man in the world able to get an erection, causing the British secret service to seize him in the name of national security in order to compel him to impregnate a select woman from every country to keep the world population thriving. There is a contest to select the lucky women and a series of wild production numbers as each bosomy winner is paraded before Percy once an hour, which is enough to wear out even the hardiest stud.

The movie ends happily with the whole world merrily fornicating its way to oblivion once male potency has been restored, making the comic point that Percy is sought after only after all of humanity has been deprived of sex for a year, and it doesn't matter how much you have so long as you can use it. Good show.

Which is more than can be said for *The Statue,* which has David Niven uncharacteristically concerned over the fact that the penis on the statue his wife Virna Lisi has sculpted of him is twice as big as his own. She refuses to tell him who it's modeled after, so he goes in search of the man, only to discover that the marble phallus was modeled after Michelangelo's "David." It's incredible that a sophisticate like Niven would lose his urbane aplomb instead of being amused or flattered by Lisi's artistic compliment to his masculinity, and it's even more incredible that any studio would finance a movie in which the humor is based on a major star's checking out male organs like an overanxious schoolboy.

Ad for Russ Meyer's Beneath the Valley of the Ultravixens *(1979), which is literally bulging with top-heavy measurements. Ken Kerr looks as though he can't make up his mind which luscious pair to grab onto first.*

151

Tim Matheson in National Lampoon's Animal House *(1978) seems to be implying something to a skeptical Verna Bloom.*

Aside from this offbeat trio of size comedies, male size jokes were rampant in movies of the 70's and 80's and still are. What is amazing about some of these references and jokes is that they occur in the oddest places. Some choice examples are as follows:

Myra Breckenridge (1970): Mae West as a Hollywood agent confronts a cowboy actor who says he is 6 feet, 7 inches. "Let's forget about the six feet," she suggestively remarks, "and concentrate on the seven inches."

The Godfather (1972): It's implied by a woman's hand gesture that Sonny Corleone (James Caan) could rival a horse.

Sex Devices (1974): At the finale of this funny softcore comedy, a wickedly grinning, swinging female kinko takes a ruler in hand to "keep track of the inches" as a stud with nine inches plunges into a horny but inexperienced young woman. A crowd looks on and cheers as the whole scene is broadcast on an X-rated radio talk show.

Teresa the Thief (1974): Monica Vitti as the rowdy Teresa rejects a drunken would-be lover by telling him his rival is hung "like a salami."

The Big Bird Cage (1972): Seedy revolutionary Sid Haig bribes his way into a female prison camp in Manila to rescue his lover by telling a gay Spanish guard—while they are peeing—that he's "a size 9½."

Great! (1975): The musical highlight of Bob Godfrey's Oscar-winning animated homage to British architect Isambard Kingdom Brunel is a bouncy double entendre song called "An Incredibly Long Top Hat."

Lisztomania (1975): Roger Daltry as Liszt has a nightmare in which his 10-foot papier mâché penis is guillotined by the women he has bedded.

The First Nudie Musical (1976): Features a sequence in which a seedy actor named Henry Schlong (Jerry Hoffman) shows up for duty as a "stunt cock." The joke is that he has a perpetual foot-long erection. Mexican spitfire Diana Canova gasps, "Eets so beeg!" To which script girl Kathleen Hietala replies, "I know. Don't you wish you had someone like him? I certainly do." There's also a hilariously phallic production number called *The Dancing Dildos.*

X-Rated Alice in Wonderland (1976): Alice (Kristine DeBell) asks the Mad Hatter if the measurement written on his hat (9⅞) is the size of his head.

The hookers in Vice Squad *(1982) talk shop, including tales about size.*

153

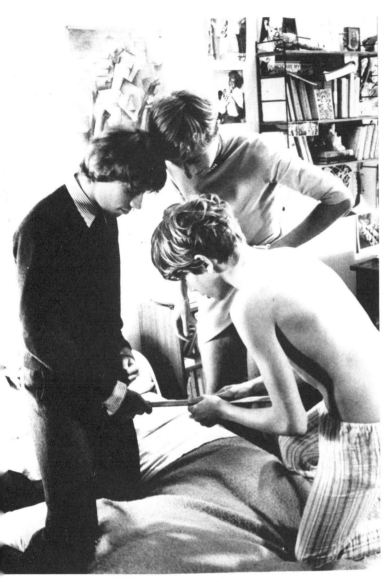

Three teenagers in Murmur of the Heart *(1971) get out a ruler to see whose is the biggest.*

"No," he haughtily replies, "it's the size of my thing."

Young Lady Chatterly (1977): In this timid, unarousing softcore update of the D.H. Lawrence novel, Harlee McBride (the title character) is told that the macho gardener is "big as a cucumber."

La Cage aux Folles (1979): Drag queen Michel Serrault disastrously auditions a young stud for his nightclub-owner love, Ugo Tognazzi. "Being good-looking and well-hung doesn't make you talented," Serrault laments.

Monty Python's Life of Brian (1979): Roman Emperor Pontius Pilate (Michael Pallin) makes repeated references to his buddy Biggus Dickus.

Being There (1979): A black maid tells retarded gardener Chance (Peter Sellers) that "I don't know how you're going to please a woman with that little thing of yours" as he ventures into the real world for the first time.

Starting Over (1979): Psychiatrist Charles Durning fixes a date for sister Jill Clayburgh with a tall, gangly basketball player, telling her in front of him that everything about him is outsized. "And is it?" asks Durning's wife, Frances Sternhagen. "Yes," the ball player smilingly replies.

Body Heat (1981): Lawyer William Hurt fears that the little girl who saw him being serviced by his aunt, Kathleen Turner, will identify him as the murderer of Turner's macho husband, Richard Crenna. It turns out that all she saw in the dark, according to D.A. Ted Danson, was something "bald, glistening and 7 or 8 inches long."

Loose Shoes (1981): In this parody of movie trailers, a *Wizard of Oz* midget (Billy Curtis) says of a scarecrow, "He *is* well-hung, isn't he?" And a black song-and-dance man warbles, "Better keep your daughters away unless you know the truth, that I'm horny as hell and I'm really hung."

Porky's (1982) and *Porky's II: The Next Day* (1983): In these raunchy hit comedies, the character named Pee Wee (Dan Monahan) is so concerned with his size that he measures himself first thing every morning, keeping track of his progress or lack of it on a growth chart. Meanwhile, the Big Man on Campus is literally that, a hulking hunk named Meat (Tony Ganios).

Star 80 (1983): Stud show MC Sandy Woshlin concludes a dong parade by exclaiming, "Hey ladies, what do you think of all our beautiful, well-hung young men?" as the women in the crowd go wild.

Spetters (1983): Three studs vying for the affection of the same girl have a measuring contest, the one with the biggest getting the prize of asking her for a date.

Two young boys at a Danish School in You Are Not Alone *(1978) check each other out in the shower. (Courtesy Award Films)*

Bachelor Party (1984): A male stripper (à la Chippendales) is asked to play a joke on some visiting ladies (bride, mother of the bride, etc.) His nickname is "Nick the Dick" and he presents his organ inside a foot-long hot dog bun. It's all some teenaged girls can do to prevent one of their overexcited mothers from ravishing the guy.

Splash (1984): In this otherwise pure romantic comedy, John Candy hoaxes his way into a scientific lab by pretending to be a member of the staff. He tells the Swedish-speaking guard, "Hey, babe. I've got a 12-inch penis." For some reason this is supposed to—and does—convince the guard that Candy is a Swedish scientist.

The Sure Thing (1985): In his creative writing class, student John Cusak hands the wrong piece of paper to teacher Viveca Lindfors, who reads it out loud. It says, in part, "I don't mean to boast, but I am well-equipped with ten inches of meaty manhood." Lindfors and the class find this snickeringly funny, much to Cusak's mortification.

Prizzi's Honor (1985): In defense of her renewed relationship with ex-lover Jack Nicholson, Angelica Huston tells her estranged father, "He took me by force. You should see the size of him."

As you can tell from this sampling of a much larger inventory of references, the size mentions are usually intended to titillate rather than dwell on the obvious. They may provoke discomfort or mild em-

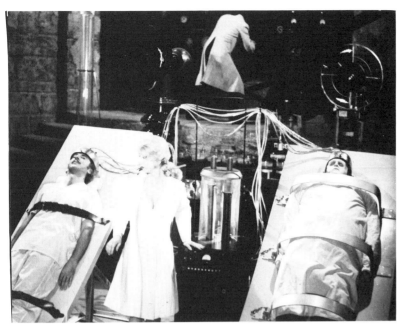

In Young Frankenstein *(1974), Teri Garr eagerly prepares Gene Wilder (left) and Peter Boyle to exchange brain cells and* schwanstückers.

Known in England as Percy's Progress, It's Not the Size That Counts *(1974) was as cheerfully ribald as this cute, clever, outrageous ad art implies.*

barrassment at worst, but they *do* get a rise out of the audience.

The all-time champ at getting that rise—because he knows it's sure-fire—is Mel Brooks. Large size is a theme to which he fearlessly keeps returning, with Madeline Kahn as his resident size queen. Brooks's comedy, of course, derives largely from low vaudeville humor where big penises and breasts always get big laughs. His two biggest-grossing movies, *Blazing Saddles* and *Young Frankenstein* (both 1974) are a testament to that, as is his biggest flop, *History of the World: Part One* (1981).

The characters Kahn plays in all three films provocatively complement each other because they are all comic depictions of nymphomania: latent, blatant and incipient. As Lili von Shtupp in *Blazing Saddles,* she is a jaded whore (incipient) whose worn-out passion is revived by the well-endowed black Sheriff Bart (Cleavon Little).

In *Young Frankenstein,* she is a prim and frigid virgin (latent) who won't let her equally prim fiancé, Dr. Victor Frankenstein (Gene Wilder), muss her hair, let alone her dress. But, when she is confronted by the primitive and rapacious monster (Peter Boyle) with his huge schwanstücker (German for "tail for sticking"), she lets herself go, belting out a chorus of "Ah, Sweet Mystery of Life." The joke is compounded when Kahn and Boyle light up cigarettes after a heavy bout of sex. Kahn has met her match in a primal hunk of man who doesn't play prudish games, but grabs for the solid gold ring of sex at the first opportunity.

Finally, Kahn plays Princess Nympho (blatant) in the Roman Empire sequence of *History of the World.* As always, she measures her men in inches. When she chooses some studs for the Midnight Orgy from 30 naked officers of the guard, she makes her selections based on their limp sexual equipment, judging her potential lovers by what they *seem* to have, not how well they may or may not use it.

Of the three comedies, *Young Frankenstein* has the best running gag because it is used to resolve the plot and drive home a thematic point. In the final reel, when Boyle and Wilder exchange brain cells in an electronic transfer, they also trade schwanzes. Now it is Wilder's wife, Teri Garr, who sings a song on their wedding night, while Kahn has to make do with a brainier but less physically-endowed monster. It is the more lustful Wilder who now has the best of both worlds: intellect and size in equal measure. Brooks would seem to be saying that as our sexual appetite and maturity grows, so do our organs; we are as well-endowed as we think we are.

Which is precisely the point being made by all of these size comedies and throwaway jokes: the less you worry about what you have and the more you use it,

the better off and happier you will be. But, as long as millions of men continue to worry needlessly about the stature of their manhood when they *should* be concerned with their stature as people and their ability as lovers, movie makers will continue to jest and taunt them about their pointless fear, making them laugh about it, which is always good, potent medicine.

Movies that emphasize huge-breasted women can't claim to be making any such point because female measurements are literally a large part of their commercial appeal. But what movies like *The Big Bird Cage, Up!, Hot T-Shirts* and other jiggle movies lack in subtlety or statement, they certainly make up for in good old-fashioned sleazy prurience. That sells tickets

too, and so long as women's measurements continue to matter to millions of men beyond all reason, they'll keep *on* selling tickets.

Just as male porno stars vie to see who is biggest, female stars, both in porno and exploitation films, compete for billing and stardom with topside measurements. Whether it's above or below the waist, it *is* the size that counts at the movies.

157

Chapter 11
BLACK EXPLOITATION

"All that talk about Black Power and Black is Beautiful, and when they finally get their long-delayed screen time, all they do is show that Black is Ugly—just as ugly as everybody else."—from Stanley Kauffmann's review of *The Mack*, in *The New Republic*.

For what seemed like forever, black actors were relegated to minor, bumbling, shuffling, stereotypical sidekick roles in hundreds of Hollywood movies. America the beautiful as seen in American movies was gleaming white and any hint that blacks were part of the proverbial American dream, let alone equal to white movie stars, was barred from the screen by racist movie producers who were fearful of offending equally racist audiences. For once, the Hays Code could not be blamed because its provisions had nothing to do with race, only with sex, drugs, violence, crime and religion.

When blacks finally got their long overdue chance to make commercial black movies, it wasn't so much because civil rights and black culture were at the center of national attention as because Hollywood loves to imitate its successes by surfing with a trend and milking a proven formula to death—in this case violent urban crime dramas. For all the agitation for a

piece of the Hollywood action by black talent, all that black producers, directors and writers could think to depict were the most vile and degrading aspects of ghetto life: pimps, prostitutes, hustlers, hit men, drug pushers, small-time gangsters, Saturday night brawls and the sexual mythology that black men are bigger, better, more macho lovers than white men.

Though the well-intended but commercially failed racial drama *The Liberation of L.B. Jones* (1970) was technically the first in the cycle, it was *Cotton Comes to Harlem* (1970) and *Shaft* (1971) that made Black Power box-office. Looking at them today, it's easy to see why they ignited the imaginations of young black audiences.

The heroes of *Cotton Comes to Harlem* are streetwise black cops Godfrey Cambridge and Raymond St. Jacques. A popular stand-up comic, Cambridge relied on his caustic wit to save the day while St. Jacques put his faith in his fists. They were

hip plainclothesmen going after black crooks, making
fools of their white superiors and playing all the
macho intimidation games that white cops had played
in movies for decades. The milieu, con game story and
realistic-seeming characters were right-on for the
times, and it was also a plus that director Ossie Davis
imbued the movie with the tangible look and feel of
contemporary ghetto life.

Richard Roundtree's *Shaft,* on the other hand, was
Super Nigger, a black fantasy combo of Sam Spade and
James Bond: hip, streetwise, angry, violent and sexy;
quick on the trigger, mean with his fists (he never got
mussed, hurt or scarred) and dynamite in bed, especially with white chicks. (Though the one in *Shaft*
complains that "You're great in the sack but you're a
shitty guy afterward.") Roundtree wasn't handsome or
a good actor, but he had presence and gave black
audiences a hero to cheer as he blew away the hoods
with his hefty phallic magnum and stood up to The
Man in New York City.

Today, *Cotton Comes to Harlem* remains a crudely enjoyable if absurd cop drama, while *Shaft* moves
like molasses and has some atrocious acting. Gordon
Parks's eye for imagery shows in every frame but his
direction is filled with deadly pauses, as though the
actors are waiting for their cues. *Shaft* is beautifully
photographed trash.

Regardless of their relative artistic merits, both
movies appealed to black and white audiences for
their hip urban settings, characters and violence, so

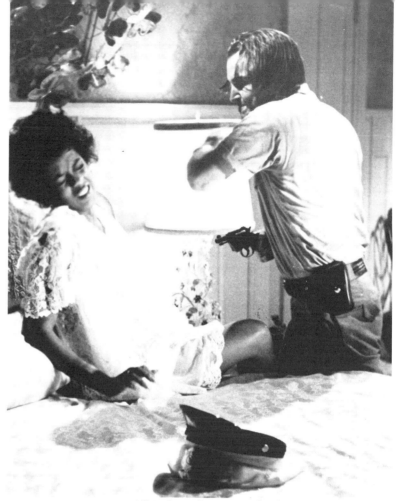

*All Lola Falana gets for her involvement
with bigot cop Anthony Zerbe in* The Liberation of L.B. Jones *(1970) is a smack upside
the head.*

Judy Pace tempts the law in
Cotton Comes to Harlem *(1970).*

Richard Roundtree in the Shaft series was the black answer to James Bond. He was invincible and he always got the girl. In Shaft's Big Score (1972), his woman was Rosalind Miles.

In Shaft in Africa (1973), it was Vonette McGee. In both movies, he barely had time to demonstrate his black sexual prowess before leaping back into blazing action to whomp the bad guys, black and white.

they were followed immediately by sequels: the tamer and far less profitable *Come Back, Charleston Blue* (1971), reteaming Cambridge and St. Jacques; and two *Shaft* sequels, *Shaft's Big Score* (1972) and *Shaft in Africa* (1973), each one sexier and more violent than the original, but just as awful. There was also a short-lived *Shaft* TV series during the 1973-74 season.

Black actor/writer/director Melvin Van Peebles was also making the rounds at this time with *Watermelon Man* (1970) and *Sweet Sweetback's Badaassss Song* (1971). The former is a one-note joke scripted by Herman Raucher: bigoted white insurance salesman Godfrey Cambridge (unconvincing as a white man) turns black overnight, causing his life to go upside down for the worse. What could have been a raucous satire was ruined by cheap, tacky production values, clichéd gags, heavy-handed message songs and some atrocious acting. The one strong scene when Cambridge sarcastically derides his racist neighbors is undercut by awful character actors who sound as though they're having trouble reading cue cards. The movie made money despite these flaws because its timing and star were right, but Van Peebles had to go begging for cash to finance *Sweet Sweetback's Badaasss Song*.

In that film, Van Peebles unleashed the full fury of an angry black man bent on getting even with white racist America. *Sweet Sweetback* emerged as a jagged black racist diatribe in which Van Peebles played a sex show stud on the run from white cops, wasting no verbal or visual opportunities to show his contempt for whitey or play up to black sexual mythology. It became a cause célèbre for its openly black sexuality and Van Peebles seemed on the verge of becoming a major black director, but he eventually went nowhere, though *Sweet Sweetback* is now circulating on home video. Today, Van Peebles is a Wall Street investment counselor and the author of a book on the stock market.

Despite the fact that the initial wave of successful exploitation films showed black cops and detectives triumphant over ghetto scum and white men, other movies in the cycle reversed that trend, making pimps, gangsters and dope peddlers the role models for black youths to emulate. This led critic Stanley Kauffmann to complain that "black filmmakers and actors, financed and industrially aided by whites, are so willing to exploit their own people … just because those examples will bring 'em in at the box office."

Black writers, directors and actors, many of whom had little or no talent, righteously protested that these were the only kinds of movies the Hollywood establishment would let them make, the same excuse used

White businessman turned black outcast Godfrey Cambridge is now a turn-off to wife Estelle Parsons in Watermelon Man *(1970).*

by the people who made the teen exploitation films of the late 70's through the late 80's. The truth was that black filmmakers seized on the commercial trend of the moment to make as much money as they could. After all, no one was forcing them to crank out those movies.

So, what we got was a hypocritical bunch of black exploitation films, most of them wretchedly made. They either glorified black criminality as the only way to triumph over whitey and rise above or escape the ghetto, or they enacted a vendetta against *white* gangsters to show their solidarity with the positive aspects of the black community. Movies like *Superfly* and *Black Caesar* in 1972 and *The Mack* and *Hell Up in Harlem* in 1973 said that if you sell enough dope, murder enough white cops and black gangsters, prostitute enough women, and show that you're bigger and badder than everyone else, you too can be the main man of the local slum. In the Super Black Chick movies like *Coffy* (1973) and *Foxy Brown* (1974) with Pam Grier and *Cleopatra Jones* (1974) with Amazonian Tamara Dobson, the characters pretended to avenge themselves and their black kin against the evil white drug pushers, but it was all part of the same crass masquerade: violence, vengeance, vigilantes, dope and hookers, laced with crude sex, vulgarity and blind hatred for honkies.

Former athlete, Jim Brown, hit it big as an ex-Green Beret out to waste the mob in Slaughter *(1972). (Courtesy Eric Hoffman)*

These raw images of a weak, divided black nation within a nation were not how black leaders wanted the public to see their people because such images were ultimately detrimental to their cause.

Ron O'Neal in *Superfly* is a perfect example of this ugly Super Spade anti-hero stereotype. He plays a pusher who wants to make that one last big cocaine sale to buy his way out of the ghetto. This means that 40 kilos of coke have to be sold to addicts and potential addicts, most of them black. For all his blather about noble intentions, O'Neal's character never addresses the fact that all that dope has to be bought by a lot of people, all of whom will be physically ravaged by the stuff. (For all his own coke snorting, O'Neal shows no ill effects.) The price of his freedom is the addictive slavery of his black brothers. Or didn't that bother O'Neal when he made the movie?

Dope pusher Ron O'Neal in Superfly *(1971) takes time out from drug peddling for some bathtub sex.*

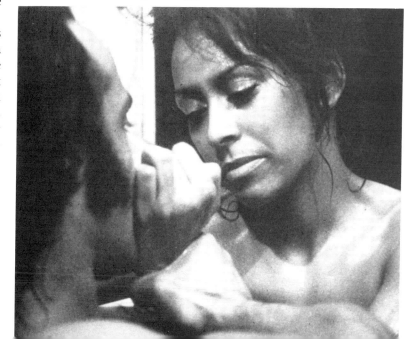

CHICKS IN CHAINS

...on the lam from a prison hell--
manacled together by hate and
the strange ideas a woman
gets after 1,000 nights
without a man.

BLACK MAMA

WHITE MAMA

| R | RESTRICTED Under 17 Requires Accompanying Parent or Adult Guardian |

four associates, ltd. presents
an american international release "**BLACK MAMA, WHITE MAMA**" starring **pam grier · margaret markov**

co-starring sid haig · lynn borden · zaldy zshornack · laurie burton · music composed and conducted by harry betts   color by movielab
produced by john ashley and eddie romero · directed by eddie romero · screenplay by h. r. christian · story by joseph viola and jonathan demme

*The worst black actress but the busiest was
Pam Grier who got her start in women-in-
chains films like* Black Mama, White Mama
(1973), an exploitation version of The
Defiant Ones. *(Courtesy Eric Hoffman)*

Another complaint about these movies was that most of their black leads could not act. This was certainly true of Fred Williamson in *Black Caesar* and *Hell Up in Harlem*. He had presence but no range or credibility. And Richard Roundtree as Shaft mostly scowled to show he was angry and concerned. Tamara Dobson as the female James Bond of *Cleopatra Jones* was tall and sexy and deft at karate chopping but nothing else. (*Kentucky Fried Movie* did a marvelous parody of *Cleopatra Jones* called *Cleopatra Schwartz* in which Marilyn Joie joins forces with a hassidic rabbi to off the badass niggers and honky pigs.) But the worst by far was Pam Grier, who was awkward and wooden in *Coffy* and *Foxy Brown*. She got better years

But who graduated to vengeance films like Coffy *(1973), in which she took aim at mobsters who turned her sister into a junkie, but managed to find time for some sex with Booker Bradshaw. (Courtesy Eric Hoffman)*

BLOODSUCKER!
Deadlier than Dracula!

His Habits...
UNSPEAKABLE
His Lusts...
INSATIABLE
His Fate...
UNBEARABLE

"'BLACULA' IS THE MOST HORRIFYING FILM OF THE DECADE."
— Count Dracula Society

BLACULA

COLOR BY MOVIELAB

An AMERICAN INTERNATIONAL Picture

PG PARENTAL GUIDANCE
May not be suitable
for pre-teenagers

SAMUEL Z. ARKOFF PRESENTS
"BLACULA" STARRING WILLIAM MARSHALL · DENISE NICHOLAS · VONETTA McGEE
GORDON PINSENT AND THALMUS RASULALA CO-STARRING EMILY LANCE CHARLES
AS GORDON YANCY · TAYLOR, Sr. AND MACAULAY AS DRACULA
PRODUCED BY JOSEPH T. NAAR DIRECTED BY WILLIAM CRAIN WRITTEN BY JOAN TORRES AND RAYMOND KOENIG MUSIC COMPOSED AND CONDUCTED BY GENE PAGE

Even a fine actor like William Marshall succumbed to the quick money of a blaxploitation flick, here keeping a straight face as he sinks his fangs into a white victim in Blacula *(1972). (Courtesy Eric Hoffman)*

later, but except for her sultry turn as a revolutionary in *The Big Bird Cage* (1972), her exploitation roles are terrible.

The one movie made during this period that reflected, in part, the reality of ghetto family life, was *Claudine* (1974), which had a double thematic edge. On the one hand, it condemned the supreme hypocrisy of a welfare system that's supposed to help struggling black families but which threatens to cut off widow Diahann Carroll's monthly checks if she marries James Earl Jones because remarriage will presumably raise her family's living standards; on the other it focused on Jones's reluctance to marry Carroll in any case for fear of commitment to her and her children. Twelve years later, *Claudine* is still relevant to an extent but dated by the fact that a growing number of black families are fatherless because the children were abandoned by teenage and young adult black men before they were even born. This means that a large percentage of teen and young adult black women who are not emotionally or financially equipped to raise a family by themselves must do so anyway. This is according to a 1986 CBS documentary *The Vanishing Family: Crisis in Black America,* in which Bill Moyers candidly talked with black teens and adults about this problem. There is abundant material here for a *Claudine* for the 80's (and a better movie than *Claudine* is), but you won't see any filmmakers, black or white, rushing to make it because it wouldn't be deemed commercial.

The one movie to defy the blaxploitation cycle with an uplifting look at a supportive black family was Martin Ritt's *Sounder* (1972), which took a naturalistic if romanticized look at the plight of black sharecroppers in 1933 Louisiana. *Sounder* is romantic in that the poverty endured by Paul Winfield and Cicely Tyson and their children seems to be less the result of racial inequality—though there are hints of that too—than the hard times suffered by all during the Depression. Racist overtones are kept to a minimum by Ritt, whose intent was to portray a black family so dimensionally that we forget their skin color and concentrate on their qualities as a loving, concerned, unified group, particularly the father-son relationship of Winfield and Kevin Hooks, which is one of the warmest ever seen on screen regardless of race.

There is also an underlying social message in *Sounder,* quietly but effectively stated by Winfield in the last reel when he cautions Hooks not to let himself be browbeaten "by them bastards" who run the social system, but to get away from the farm to a better way of life as soon as he is able. Compare this to the vitriolic soapboxes of the blaxploitation films—in

Welfare mother Diahann Carroll in Claudine *(1974) was also raising a family, hoping that James Earl Jones would become the husband she longs for and the father her unruly kids desperately need.*

Diana Ross and Tony Perkins look utterly bored as would-be lovers in Mahogany *(1975). And this was one of the more romantic blaxploitation flicks.*

Amid all the cruelly cynical and violent blaxploitation films of the early 70's, there was Sounder *(1972) with its uplifting depiction of familial love and togetherness. Here Paul Winfield and Cicely Tyson return with their kids (that's Kevin Hooks at the right) from a family outing.*

which the black "heroes" exhort their followers to "off the white honkies"—and you can see which approach is the more maturely human and thus more moving and inspiring.

For all of their positive and well-intended qualities, though—*Sounder* much more so than the generally superficial *Claudine*—both movies were bloodless and therefore less hugely profitable exceptions in a link of cinematic sausages that grew progressively vicious in outlook.

The only glamour in the genre was provided by Diana Ross and Billy Dee Williams in *Lady Sings the Blues* (1972) and *Mahogany* (1975). The former was a black version of a clichéd Hollywood musical biography, presenting a distorted fictionalization of the life of

Dapper, handsome Billy Dee Williams goes strutting with his lady, Marcia McBroom, in The Bingo Long Traveling All-Stars and Motor Kings *(1976).*

blues singer Billie Holiday. It was popular anyway because of the chemistry between Ross and Williams, who seemed on the verge of becoming the black Clark Gable. *Mahogany* was an even soggier romantic contrivance about a fashion designer and a Chicago political activist. Both movies were box-office hits, but despite *Mahogany's* take, the blaxploitation cycle was at an end, having burned itself out through a sheer glut of cynically made bad movies. You can only capitalize on a formula for so long until even the audience it's aimed at grows weary of the repetition.

More to the point, black audiences were sick of seeing so many negative images of themselves, preferring instead the hip familial humor of *Good Times,* and the upwardly mobile plot machinations of *The Jeffer-*

sons—an updated Amos 'n' Andy—both on television and both produced by Norman Lear.

The black exploitation cycle produced nothing of lasting value during the five years it operated. The movies that got made captured the militant black mood of the time, but they also exchanged one set of corrupt, demeaning stereotypes for another. They certainly avoided any real insights into black people or into the volatile class and culture struggles between white and black America. Black critics can argue that the racial animosity of these films was an inevitable outgrowth of decades of suppressed black talent, but hatred only breeds hatred and if black is beautiful, why not show it? If even a few of these movies had risen above calculating ghetto cynicism, had reached

Homecoming Vietnam veteran Richard Pryor in Some Kind of Hero *(1981) greets his long-waiting wife only to learn she has divorced him and remarried.*

So he takes solace with simpatico hooker Margot Kidder instead. A rare black/white sexual combo in mainstream American movies.

into the depths of the black character as the best of the black poets do—Langston Hughes was dead-on when he wrote about "a dream deferred"—and as *Sounder* certainly did, the cycle might have had a lasting and profoundly positive impact on the way Hollywood movies use and treat blacks.

As it was, there were very few first-rate black actors rising to the top in mainstream "A" movies from the late 1970's to the mid-80's, men and women who could make a positive difference by creating a roster of black stars equal in stature, ability and commercial popularity to white stars.

The few black stars who emerged included:

—Richard Pryor in *Silver Streak* (1976) and *Stir Crazy* (1980) with Gene Wilder as a salt-and-pepper comedy team, and in the comedy-drama *Some Kind of Hero* (1982) as a returning Vietnam veteran whose civilian life crumbles around him. In that movie, he had some semi-explicit sex scenes with white actress Margot Kidder, and that in itself was a minor cinematic landmark because the relationship is a simpatico one, not abusive as would have been the case in blaxploitation.

—Billy Dee Williams as a brash young ballplayer in 1939 who forms his own razzle-dazzle black ball team in *The Bingo Long Traveling All-Stars and Motor Kings* (1976), and as Lando Kalrisian in *The Empire Strikes Back* (1980) and *Return of the Jedi* (1983).

—Louis Gossett, Jr., as a tough drill sergeant in *An Officer and a Gentleman* (1981, winning an Oscar as Best Supporting Actor), and as a lizard-like alien in *Enemy Mine* (1985).

—Tapdancing superstar Gregory Hines as a charismatic tapdancer in both *The Cotton Club* (1984) and *White Nights* (1985), the latter opposite Mikhail Baryshnikov.

—And the biggest black star of all to emerge in the 1980's: glib, brash, raucous, irreverent, street smart, hilariously vulgar Eddie Murphy in such monster comedy hits as *48 Hours* (1982), *Trading Places* (1983), and *Beverly Hills Cop* (1984). The latter two are especially noteworthy because they're among the few black starring movies in years that didn't depend on a white sidekick or partner for the movie to appeal to white audiences.

But for all the commercial success of most of these movies, and the splendid acting range shown by their black stars and co-stars, few of them involved romance or sex for these black actors, and certainly not with white women with the occasional exception of a minor movie like *Some Kind of Hero*. For all of *his* comic charisma and commercial clout, Eddie Murphy is *not* a romantic star.

Ironically, the one nearly all-black major Hollywood movie of the mid-1980's with sexual subthemes was made by white producer-director Steven Spielberg because he alone had the commercial clout to make a movie of Alice Walker's Pulitzer Prize-winning rural, feminist, period novel *The Color Purple*. A saga that follows a subjugated black woman (Whoopi Goldberg) through over 30 years of adversity and jubilant triumph, *The Color Purple* (1985) touched on incest, sexual slavery, lesbianism, unwed pregnancy and other sexual themes.

Though few people, including Spielberg, thought the movie would do more than break even commercially, it turned out that audiences loved the movie and cheered Whoopi Goldberg, who is incandescent as the ultimately victorious Celie. The movie also generated a torrent of critical controversy over Spielberg's polished adaptation of the Walker novel—some felt the movie was lyrically true to the book's spirit while others saw it as a side-stepping cop-out on its darker aspects—and drew a howl of protest from black male civic leaders because it portrays black men, in the early part of this century (and, by extension, today), as fools, incompetents and sexual monsters: there isn't one decent black male in this movie. You could say that this too was a form of racial stereotyping, but after all, *The Color Purple is* the story of one woman's life journey seen through her eyes.

The Color Purple *(1985): Margaret Avery likes the way Danny Glover makes love...*

...but her most passionate friendship and love are reserved for Glover's subjugated wife Whoopi Golberg, who glows under Avery's touch. Or rather we would see her glow if director Steven Spielberg had dared to go beyond this mere hint of lesbian love.

The truth is that after years of seeing black women play mainly subservient roles in movies—as white women had done for decades—it was thrilling to see Goldberg, Oprah Winfrey and Margaret Avery (as gifted a trio of actresses, black or white, as we've seen in years) band together as black sisters in triumph over their foolish, pig-headed black brethren. For a change, and this was also a point of controversy, the male roles were subservient and counterpoint to the female leads, which also included Desreta Jackson in a heart-rending performance as the brutalized young Celie.

Goldberg's grownup Celie, in particular, is a revelation. Hers is a masterful portrayal of sheer domestic competence, female solidarity (just watch the scene in the dry goods store where she wordlessly lends a defeated Winfrey a helping sisterly hand), and blossoming, take-charge womanliness. This is a performance that glows with an inner fire. The one thing wrong with and missing from the role, and the movie, as many critics have rightly pointed out, is Celie's

crucial lesbian relationship with dance hall vamp Shug Avery (Avery), which was sidestepped by Spielberg and screenwriter Menno Meyjes in favor of a less provocative and thereby less fully dimensional narrative. Because the movie only hints at this female love affair before ignoring it altogether, we are robbed of a more complete involvement in and insight into the dramatic changes in Celie's character over the years. We get the emotional side of the Celie/Shug friendship, but not the physically loving one, for fear of alienating the mass audience.

Despite this flaw and others, *The Color Purple* in one fell swoop has brought us a new generation of black movie stars—including Danny Glover as the handsome, tyrannical and ignorant Mr.—actors we can look forward to seeing in many movies in the years to come. Actors who, because of the movie's resounding commercial success, will appeal to racially mixed audiences, just as Eddie Murphy does. In fact, given Murphy's multi-racial appeal as a comic actor, and Goldberg's own comic gift, there is no good reason

Black mating dance: The "Creole Love Song" production number from The Cotton Club *(1984).*

why they couldn't or shouldn't co-star in a romantic comedy. With the right script and director, and with a solid supporting cast, they could easily become the 80's and 90's black equivalent of Tracy and Hepburn.

In short, with a gallery of first-rate black actors and actresses to choose from who have proven sex appeal, Hollywood producers have no excuse not to live up to their perennial lip service of racial quality by using these performers in other uplifting mass audience movies worthy of their wide-ranging talents. If a fine actor like Bill Cosby can star in the top-rated show on network television—and one of the warmest, wittiest, sexiest and most intelligent—there is no good reason why other blacks cannot command lead roles in a string of intelligent, witty, sexy, dynamic blockbuster movies, and quiet masterworks too.

The time is now.

Chapter 12
TEEN EXPLOITATION

"The best one can say about *Paradise Motel* is that the actors and director have at least not disgraced themselves in a movie genre where disgrace, offensiveness, shallowness, mercenary slickness and crass witlessness have become the order of the day."—From Michael Wilmington's review of *Paradise Motel* in the *Los Angeles Times*.

"You booze, you dope, you sleep with whoever. I don't even know who you are. You look like kids but you don't act like them. You're short 40-year-olds and you're tough ones."—Sally Kellerman to Jodie Foster in *Foxes*.

"No one ever went broke underestimating the intelligence of the American public."—H.L. Mencken

It's no secret that teenagers comprise a large percentage of ticket-buying moviegoers. Hollywood has always catered to the dating crowd, to what it thinks teenagers and young adults want to see at the local theater or drive-in, even if the end results have little or nothing to do with what teenagers really look like, say, think about and do. Frankie Avalon and Annette Funicello were the reigning teen idols of the 1960's, cranking out a platoon of *Beach Party* movies, even though they must have been the oldest "teens" on record. Much of what passes for teen entertainment these days are really post-Code variations and updates of the proven farcical formulae of those "old" movies.

Today's movie studio executives have it firmly implanted in their vacuously commercial minds that what teen audiences want to see most of all are wild parties ending in food fights, endless reels of naked tits-and-ass, horny teenagers neurotically obsessed with getting laid, mean-spirited pranks aimed at car-

toonish high school and college authorities, and an absolute, flagrant disregard for what high schools are supposed to be all about: getting an education.

Since 1978, there has been an onslaught of teen exploitation movies that are deliberately, willfully bad. In a series of articles for the *Los Angeles Times* in 1985 entitled "Dumb Movies," Peter H. Brown outlined the specific formula for these films, making it clear that studio heads are insisting on the worst possible movies that writers and directors can conjure up—the raunch syndrome—to make the biggest piles of money from teen audiences before they finally tire of the game just as black audiences did with the blaxploitation films of the early 70's. Of course, by making these movies such colossal commercial hits, teenagers are saying that they love this brainless junk and cannot get enough of it. These are vacation-time films and almost anything remotely reeking of intelligence is shunned by them.

The two movies that were the catalyst for this craze were *National Lampoon's Animal House* and *Grease* in 1978. What made *Animal House* work for audiences was that it was set in the early 1960's, giving it a nostalgic distance, and made bawdy fun of college education and fraternity life. If you examine *Animal House* schematically, you'll find that it's just a series of disconnected gag sequences with a modicum of characterization; just enough to make us identify with Delta House bums like Peter Riegert, campus stud Tim Matheson and campus slob John Belushi. (Somehow Belushi is coasting by with an F+.) There are isolated clever or funny bits, mainly sexual ones like a prom queen masturbating a preppie with a plastic glove, but no cohesive, building storyline escalating to a climactic comic payoff. Even the parade finale is just more mindless demolition. What made it commercially successful, though, *was* its bawdy humor, its implied sex and collegiate underdogs the audience could root for.

Grease went back a bit further for *its* mindless nostalgia: to the late 1950's, though it doesn't have an authentic 50's ring to it, does not resound with the culture of the time except for a well-choreographed American Bandstand takeoff. What it *does* have are John Travolta's swaggeringly macho sex appeal and Olivia Newton-John's sweetly innocent love for Travolta which turns into black-garbed sluttishness in the final reel. *Grease* reeks of leering, sneaky sex throughout, and that, along with its star power and aggregation of insipid pseudo-50's "rock" songs, made it a blockbuster hit. Actually, it's a 60's *Beach Party* movie in 50's garb.

This finger-snapping foursome, despite looking a decade or more older than they were playing, made Grease *(1978) the most commercially successful movie musical of all time. Left to right: Jeff Conaway, Olivia Newton-John, John Travolta and Stockard Channing.*

Bevies of beauties are an integral part of the teen movie formula. Bill Murray is surrounded by them in the raucous camp comedy Meatballs *(1979). From left to right, they are: Cindy Girling, Margot Pinvidic, Sarah Torgov, Norma Dell'Agnese and Kristine DeBell. (Courtesy Peter H. Brown)*

Faced with the monumental box office receipts of these two movies, and a few other teen sex comedies, studio executives could do only one thing: cash in on this new craze with more, much more of the same, using a formula of low budgets plus imbecilic scripts equals high yields. It paid off with a vengeance in a series of teen exploitation films that not only rank among the worst movies of the last ten years but among the worst ever made anywhere. The dishonor roll is as long as your arm and includes:

—*Teen Lust* and *Goin' All the Way* in 1978;

—*Swim Team* and *Meatballs* in 1979;

—*Private Lessons, Lunch Wagon* and the Brooke Shields desert island make-out movie *The Blue Lagoon* in 1980;

—*Stripes* (a 50's-style army comedy with an 80's-style nose-thumbing sensibility), *Final Exam* and *Student Bodies* in 1981, the latter two being stalk-and-slash horror movies aimed at teens;

—*Grease II* (one of the few bad ones that bombed), *Zapped, The Last American Virgin, Fast Times at Ridgemont High,* and *Porky's* (one of the enjoyable raunchy ones) in 1982;

—*Spring Break, Private School, Footloose, My Tutor, Joy Sticks, Valley Girl, Sixteen Candles* and *Porky's II: The Next Day* in 1983;

—*Piggy's, Weekend Pass, Meatballs II, Where the Boys Are 1984, Hot Dog: The Motion Picture* (as one critic put it, "Not to be confused with *Hot Dog: The Opera*"), *Bachelor Party* and *Revenge of the Nerds* in 1984;

—*Porky's III, Gotcha, Weird Science, Real Genius,* and *My Science Project* in 1985;

—And *Basic Training* and *Hamburger: The Motion Picture* (from the same people who gave us *Hot Dog* the you-know-what) in 1986.

This is by no means all the teen market titles released during those years, nor are all of them exactly alike or a total loss, but with few exceptions the "plots" for these exploitation quickies are fairly standardized:

A flaky crew of losers, misfits and nerds tangles with villainous adults while singlemindedly obeying their prime directive to get laid at all costs; spends as much time as possible leering at a bumper crop of luscious T&A through peep holes, video camera set-ups or conveniently open shower doors; scores with well-endowed chicks despite themselves (making you wonder about the collective intelligence of these girls); and, through a series of elaborate pranks, emerge triumphant over boobish, pompous adult authorities. All of which is set to a Dolbyized sound-track of whatever happen to be the current rock hits or rock tunes in search of a chart bullet.

Until the summer of 1985, when the exceptional

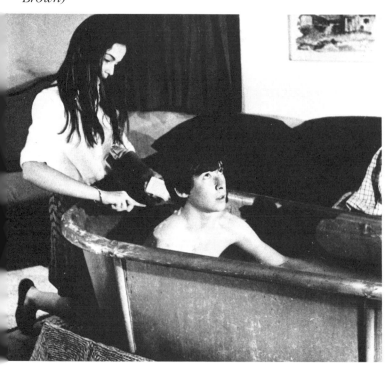

Anicee Alvina happily scrubs her runaway teen lover Sean Bury in Friends *(1971).*

A whole bunch of lusciously stacked teen foxes strut their stuff at a bikini contest in Spring Break *(1983). Cute and cuddly Jayne Modean is the one at center stage.*

Two teen nymphs give a hint of well-endowed things to come in Lunch Wagon *(1980). (Courtesy Peter H. Brown)*

Back to the Future became *the* big teen *and* adult hit, the formula obviously worked because the majority of these movies grossed a sum total of more than $1 billion on average budgets of $4-5 million, often much less. But the formula alone doesn't completely explain why all these movies combined made so much money if they're almost all so terrible. The main reasons millions of dating couples have flocked to see these sex comedies are: 1) they root for underdog heroes versus brainless hunks and pompous adults; 2) they almost all feature both male and female nudity for across the board audience titillation; 3) the sex is comic, allowing for a farcical release valve; 4) the nerdy or earthy good guys *always* win and get laid; and 5) the teen heroes are played by actors in their early to late twenties because teen audiences see themselves as older and more mature than they really are.

Mark Herrier (left) and Wyatt Knight take a leering peek into the girls' shower room in the most famous scene from the raunchy commercial hit Porky's *(1981). Kaki Hunter is the cute coed at the far right.*

As with the blaxploitation flicks, the men and women who write, produce and direct these movies protest that it's the only way they can break into the business (notwithstanding the quality movies that also get made by newcomers), that they are forced to pander to a slob mentality by venal studio executives. Of course, they're protesting all the way to the bank and their next teen movie credit, so who's kidding whom?

The quintessential teen sex comedy of the early 1980's, the one that crystallized the formula almost to a fault, was Bob Clarke's surprise hit, *Porky's* (1982). Its success was a surprise only because studio executives turned it down; in retrospect, its mass audience appeal was guaranteed. For what it's worth, *Porky's* is the best of the T&A films because it's an example of locker room humor that strikes a collective nerve. It has the ring of a man—Clarke—who recalls growing up in a teenage 1950's Southern ambience and has a hilariously vulgar cartoon quality to its sexual antics (like those *Sex to Sexty* comic books that have been around for decades) that makes it a lot of fun despite the clichés and character stereotypes it perpetuates. It's also the movie that made peep holes, shower room scenes, penis-size jokes, sexually jealous ugly women and handsome campus hunks *de rigueur* in teen movies.

Porky's II was a flavorless, calculating cash-in sequel, whereas the original, though hardly a good movie in the usual sense, had a rambunctious, spontaneous feel to it. Porky's II made money, though, which gave us the even worse Porky's III. That one was so abysmally crass and moronic even teen audiences rejected it. The best thing about all of the Porky's movies is a delightful young actress named Kaki Hunter, seen here in the shower room scene from the first Porky's. She is a sweetly sexy, warmly understanding, simpatico delight and deserves much better roles.

Ironically, for all the megabucks earned by these movies, the three best male actors to emerge in the teen market—Tom Cruise, John Cusak and Jonathan Cryer—did so in movies that transcended the raunchy youth formula with solid, human, intelligently scripted stories. That these good movies starring these young men also made money proved that teen moviegoers don't only want to see cartoonish misrepresentations of themselves.

What made these actors and their movies special? Let's take a look at them an actor at a time.

Tom Cruise soared to stardom in 1983 in Risky Business and the underrated All the Right Moves, which is a straight drama. In both movies, Cruise looks, acts and talks like a real teenager with the real interests, problems, preoccupations and sex drive of a teenager.

Moreover, he has a boyishly appealing personality that gives him star quality. Who can forget the scene in Risky Business where he lip syncs and gyrates to the tune "Give Me that Old-Time Rock and Roll," or the artfully photographed and edited sequences in which he makes love to hooker Rebecca DeMornay?

And contrast the sexual relationships in both movies. In Risky Business, Cruise's involvement with DeMornay is both erotic and fraught with peril because he turns teen pimp for her, converting his parents' home into a brothel while they're away on vacation. There is a keen edge to the sexual humor here which makes the movie involving. On the other hand, his relationship with Lea Thompson in All the Right Moves is an authentic teenage romance, a mixture of loyal friendship and recrimination over his selfish goals culminating in a beautiful bed scene that's an act of genuine erotic love.

John Cusak became the comic find of 1985 in The Sure Thing. Under Rob Reiner's expert, sure-footed comic direction, Cusak emerged as one of the most ingratiating comic maniacs of his generation, taking all sorts of wildly impromptu prankish risks, but never making a false move or losing audience sympathy for his zany character. The Sure Thing is a modern, college-based variant on It Happened One Night, teaming the uninhibited and scholastically lazy Cusak

Lovesick Tom Cruise takes hooker girlfriend Rebecca DeMornay on a romantic subway ride in Risky Business *(1983).*

And faces the future with girlfriend Lea Thompson in All the Right Moves *(1983).*

and sexually repressed classmate Daphne Zuniga as a cross-country odd couple. He is heading straight for a gorgeous blonde in California who is a sexual sure thing (his fantasies about the encounter, one of them shown here, are comic gems), she for her shallow, play-it-safe preppie lover. You know the rest.

While *The Sure Thing* overall falls a little short of being a classic, you still leave the theatre feeling exuberant because two people who are seemingly temperamental opposites, (remember *The African Queen?*) and who think they know what they want, find more in common with each other at the end, and you're happy for them. Moreover, you've been royally entertained without having your intelligence insulted, which is a rare occurrence these days.

Finally, there was Jonathan Cryer in a pleasant surprise called *No Small Affair* (1984). He is an obsessive, girl-shy shutterbug smitten with and pursuing rock singer Demi Moore. As one critic put it, Cryer is "Jerry Lewis with his IQ showing." He is spindly, vulnerable, awkward and romantically well-meaning, turning down a freebie with a sincere hooker in favor of first-time sex with a girl he loves. For these reasons,

The Sure Thing *(1985): In a fantasy scene from one of the best of the teen sex comedies, John Cusak dreams his every need is being tended to by "sure thing" Nicolette Larson.*

when the movie finally reaches the climactic love scene with Cryer and Moore, that scene is something special, full of joy, forgiveness and sensuality; a tenderly implicit love scene proving once again that less is satisfyingly more.

Other likeable teen stars include Molly Ringwald and Anthony Michael Hall in *Sixteen Candles* (1984) and *The Breakfast Club* (1985)—both directed by John Hughes—and Emilio Estevez, also in *The Breakfast Club*. The former is typically wretched exploitation fare with one good scene between Ringwald and dad Paul Dooley (who steals the show as the only intelligent adult around), while the latter is *My Dinner with Andre* for the teen set. It's a contrived character study of five hell-raising teens who spend the entire movie in Saturday school detention rapping about their mutual family and sexual problems and baring their psyches to each other. Though it's the only one of the teen films that actually settles down to *listen* to what contemporary teens are thinking and feeling—with not a beer blast or T&A scene in sight—and boasts some fine ensemble acting, *The Breakfast Club* is self-consciously well-intended with five stereotypically-based teen characters, and an overall air of artificiality and pat glibness. We know from the outset that they will emerge from their day-long enforced group therapy closer to each other and cathartically one up on the

Singer Demi Moore returns the compliment of Jonathan Cryer's sweetly sincere love by offering to make love to him in the underrated romantic comedy No Small Affair *(1984).*

Campus queen Haviland Morris has had one too many beers, leaving self-styled teen stud Anthony Michael Hall (all talk, no action) petrified of taking advantage in Sixteen Candles *(1984).*

Ally Sheedy talks about marriage with roommate Judd Nelson in St. Elmo's Fire *(1985).*

system that put them there, so where's the suspense, the sense of revelation about these teens and, by extension, the teens in the audience?

Foxes (1980) also strove for authenticity. Unlike most other teen films where the language is an offensive mixture of vulgarity and clichés, the teen gang here acts and talks like real adolescents, especially Jodie Foster who, as always, is the most grown-up of the bunch; too grown-up for her own good. *Foxes* is almost a good movie about teenage girls coming to terms with their blossoming sex drives and the boys and men in their lives, but it lacks cohesion and a plot; it's mainly a string of confrontations and sexual episodes leading to a tragic finale.

Other appealing personalities include:

—Cuddly Jayne Modean in the breezy and energetic if moronic *Spring Break*. Modean is the girl-next-door you want to hug and marry, but aside from *Spring Break,* I haven't seen her in anything but TV commercials. She should be making more movies and charming us more often with her Teddy Bear femininity.

—Foxy tigress Corinne Alphen, also in *Spring Break*. This woman has a face, bosom and body to rouse the dead and it's a shame she retired to get married after making *Spring Break,* especially since her only other claim to fame is being chosen *Penthouse* Pet of the Year twice. Here's hoping she comes back.

—Precociously mature but romantically shy Mary Stuart Masterson in *Heaven Help Us* (1985), a low-key *Animal House* set in a Catholic boys' school in the 1960's.

—Brainy but inhibited Daphne Zuniga who learned the art of cutting loose from John Cusak in *The Sure Thing.*

—And Nicholas Cage as an infatuated punk outsider in *Valley Girl*. Cage imbued a potentially shallow character with depth and sensitivity. He later co-starred in *Birdy.*

Each of these actors and actresses are superior or equal to their material, making one eager to see them all in more movies worthy of their presence and talent. Cusak, in particular, went on to star in two other movies in 1985, one of them being Disney's critically acclaimed *The Journey of Natty Gann.* Of the others, Anthony Michael Hall had the misfortune to co-star in another John Hughes teen fantasy, *Weird Science* (1985), in which he and Ian Mitchell-Smith computer-generate a living *Playboy/Penthouse* centerfold in the person of Kelly LeBrock—a wildly implausible premise that sinks into mind-numbing vulgar witlessness after LeBrock is created because Hughes doesn't know where to go from there. The best that can be said

Jodie Foster (far left) in Foxes *(1979) exchanges angry words with boyfriend Robert Romanus as sisters Marilyn Kagan (at Foster's left) and Cheri Currie (at Romanus's right) look on.*

Left to right: Kandice Stroh, Marilyn Kagan, Jodie Foster and Cherie Currie realistically portrayed Valley girls with growing pains in Foxes *(1979).*

about *Weird Science* and the other, similar-titled teen sex comedies of 1985—*Real Science* etc.—is that they all flopped, canceling each other out through sheer sameness.

I cannot talk about the teen movie idols of the last ten years without mentioning Brooke Shields, the most overhyped and overexposed of them all. Her biggest success was in *The Blue Lagoon,* a boring tropical island tease vehicle in which she was nude doubled. Shields undeniably has erotic screen presence and teen star quality, but she can't act and has a bubblegum personality: all airhead and no substance.

Likewise, this chapter cannot end without discussing one of the biggest and most appealing teen idols to emerge in the mid-80's in one of the best movies of 1985: Michael J. Fox in the delightful time-travel fantasy *Back to the Future.* Fox is what used to be called a dreamboat: a charismatic, adventuresome young man with self-confident spunk, a quizzical

Brian Backer and Jennifer Jason Leigh chastely peck in Fast Times at Ridgemont High (1982).

Mary Stuart Masterson and Andrew McCarthy share a tender moment in Heaven Help Us (1985).

Graduating female seniors in Private School (1983) bare their bottoms for a parting group shot. (Courtesy Peter H. Brown)

Jiggly coed Betsy Russell decides to have some teasing fun with Matthew Modine when he sneaks into the girls' dorm in drag in Private School (1983).

Christopher Atkins and Brooke Shields in The Blue Lagoon *(1980) are shipwrecked cousins who discover the beauty of natural love.*

Matt Dillon and Diane Lane get down to more passionate business in Rumble Fish *(1983).*

Steve Bassett in Spring Break *(1983) gets a hugful from nymph Corinne Alphen; it's easy to see why she was chosen Penthouse Pet of the Year twice.*

In Class *(1983), An-drew McCarthy is seduced by Jac-queline Bisset, not knowing she is his best friend's mother.*

This looks like a locker room scene from any one of a dozen mainstream teen sex comedies, but in fact it's from the porno block-buster Debbie Does Dallas *(1978). (Courtesy VCX Video)*

nature, and a healthy penchant for risk-taking. When he outsmarts the town bullies by pitting his skateboard prowess against their less maneuverable car, you thrill to his heroism along with Lea Thompson. And what a treat watching him "invent" rock and roll by aping Chuck Berry's chord style and trademark duck walk for "Johnny Be Good." Fox is so comfortably likeable and charming, and the movie, which is aimed at a mainstream audience, is such a rollicking good adventure, you don't want it to end. Neither did tens of millions of moviegoers who gave *Back to the Future* such a monumental repeat business that it stayed in first run for nearly a year, becoming *the* top-grossing movie of 1985.

The other exhilarating teen-appeal movie of 1985, *The Sure Thing,* also made money, though not as much as it could have according to a report in the *Los Angeles Times.* Though the movie was packing them in for six weeks early in the year, it was pulled during the peak of its word-of-mouth popularity because exhibitors felt no loyalty to Embassy, its releasing company, preferring to screen movies from other, bigger name companies already contracted for. *The Sure Thing* grossed $15.5 million on a budget of $4.5 million and another $7 million in cassette sales; hardly the flop some industry analysts made it out to be.

What all of this adds up to is that despite its worst intentions, and unlike the blaxploitation genre, the teen trend has actually given us a handful of good movies, some genuinely funny, moving and erotic moments, some shining talents to keep watching in the years to come. Moreover, the fact that teen moviegoers flocked by the millions to see *The Breakfast Club, The Sure Thing* and *Back to the Future* means that, conventional studio wisdom notwithstanding, they *are* interested in smartly done romantic comedies and cinematic gab fests that seem to be speaking to their private concerns. The cycle of raunchy prurience is still with us, but it cannot last forever, or can it?

One can only hope that the commercial success of these movies signifies that teenage moviegoers want something more from date night movies in the long run than hyperthyroid cornball comedies that misrepresent them all as sexually deranged airheads. If that finally proves to be the case in the coming years, then actors like Cage, Cruise, Cryer, Cusak, Estevez, Foster, Fox, Hall, Hunter, Masterson, Modean, Ringwald and Zuniga may have the chance to give us some of the most exciting and elevating performances American movies have seen in years.

However, any such longterm overhaul of screen content—the overthrow of dumb movies for thinking ones—has to be voted on by teenage and young adult moviegoers with their wallets, because that is the only kind of election for change that counts in Hollywood.

Chapter 13
STRAIGHT WITH CHASERS

"And when two lovers woo, they still say I love you. On that you can rely. The world will always welcome lovers as time goes by." — from *Casablanca*

For all the hype, exploitation, violent machismo, kinkiness, perversion and cheap sex that have been flooding movie screens since 1970, you might think that good old-fashioned heterosexual romance had gone out of style, that there was little room left for sweeter, more traditional couplings. It certainly seemed that way at times, but as with everything else discussed in this book, those pairings now come to us in Dolby stereo with greater verbal and visual honesty, realism and fluency, and in a wider range of emotional Technicolors.

With the abolition of the Hays/Breen code, screen lovers and married couples could kiss deeply and with genuine passion, sleep in the same bed, explore each other's bodies in minute detail while leaving the clinical mechanics of intercourse to the imagination (if the producer and/or director have any aesthetic sense), and just generally express the mental and physical attractions that operate in real life.

Two of the most popular movie love stories of the early 70's were *Friends* and *Summer of '42* (both 1971). *Friends* is forgotten now—Leonard Maltin rates it a BOMB in his *TV Movies* guide—but at the time it pleased a lot of teenagers with its Elton John score and its implausible tale of two runaway adolescents (Sean Bury and Anicee Alvina) who set up housekeeping in rural France and have a baby.

Summer of '42 lingers in the public mind because it lovingly evoked an earlier era and the teenage sexual pranks that went with it, made a brief star of lovely Jennifer O'Neill, and featured an artfully filmed love scene with her and Gary Grimes—the war widow making love to the anxious teenager because she likes him and because he's handy in her hour of grief.

The most oddball love story of the 70's was surely Hal Ashby's black comedy *Harold and Maude* (1971), starring Bud Cort as a morbid young man who delights in phony suicides, and Ruth Gordon as the much, *much* older woman with whom he falls in love

In Summer of '42 *(1971), grieving war widow Jennifer O'Neill tenderly kisses teenage Gary Grimes as a prelude to lovemaking.*

(she shares his love of funerals, for one thing). She brings Cort out of his dour shell with her love for doing impetuously crazy things and her uninhibited peppiness in bed, the generation gap be damned. But, just when it seems they are about to marry, she fatally poisons herself, presumably because she feels it's wrong to burden Cort with such an old wife. This ending rings a false note because there is no good reason why Gordon should want to die.

Harold and Maude has weathered its initial commercial and critical failure—Paramount buried it and a lot of unthinking critics didn't know what to make of it—to become a cult favorite for its offbeat romanticism and bouyant nose-thumbing at social and sexual conventions.

The most bittersweet romantic of the 70's was Woody Allen, whose wry glimpses of the complex, tragicomic world of modern and fantasy romance—usually in a New York milieu—in *Play it Again, Sam* (1972), *Sleeper* (1973), and *The Purple Rose of Cairo* (1985) touched a collective nerve with their incisive originality. Allen's best movie by far is *Annie Hall*

Diane Keaton and Woody Allen share a twilight moment in the shadow of Queensborough Bridge in Manhattan *(1979).*

(1977), which deservedly won the Oscar for Best Picture and is arguably *the* quintessential relationship movie of the 1970's.

Here, Allen crystallizes his Jewish schlemiel persona as Alvy Singer, a neurotic comedian who constantly thwarts satisfying relationships with women, including a marriage, because he doesn't feel he's worthy of them. Along comes a tall, gangly, WASP kook named Annie Hall (Diane Keaton, Allen's former real life lover) who would seem to be all wrong for him, yet they hit it off in tentative, piquant degrees. Allen shows this evolution with electrifying visual wit:

Scene: Allen and Keaton talk about everything except what's on their minds, which Allen shows us in subtitles.

Scene: As they're making love, Keaton's spirit steps back because she's not in the mood, leaving Allen with a joyless body which is not what he wants, and he says so as he bickers with the Keaton apparition.

Scene: A split screen of Allen and Keaton talking to their respective psychiatrists. Allen complains that he and Keaton seldom make love anymore, only three times a week. Keaton complains that three times a week is too much.

It's this kind of constant, lightning inventiveness that has us looking at romantic/sexual commitment with fresh eyes, making us take stock of ourselves so that we'll want to do better, be more sensitive and open in our own lives.

The use of the split screen in Annie Hall *(1977) emphasizes the literal split in the sexual relationship of Diane Keaton and Woody Allen. Three times a week is too much for her, not enough for him.*

While Hollywood was busy producing both conventional and unconventional romances, foreign filmmakers were delighting us with their own earthy exports, some of which are neglected classics.

One of them is Carlo DiPalma's excellent *Teresa the Thief* (1974), a bawdy, impudent, picaresque comedy about a thieving Italian outcast (Monica Vitti) and her various sexual escapades with ne'er-do-wells and fellow thieves over three decades as she tries to find the right rogue for her heart and loins. We live and love with this feisty paisan as she bounces from cad to cad in a sort of erotic pinball game, racking up climaxes but never scoring the final victory of the big catch, or losing hope that she will.

Oddly enough, *Teresa the Thief* played only briefly in the United States in the late 70's and hasn't been seen since. This is both inexplicable and a bloody shame because its superb production values, swooning Nino Rota score and lusty, bravura, full-throttle performance by Vitti make the movie a thoroughgoing delight.

Another unseen gem from 1974 is the Brazilian *The Truce,* nominated for a Best Foreign Film Oscar, but seen in Los Angeles, at least, only once at Filmex. It's the story of a widowed middle-aged businessman

Rowdy Monica Vitti as Teresa the Thief *(1974) hopes a bit of affectionate lathering will help keep her latest lover around awhile.*

Middle-aged, middle-class businessman Hector Alterio finds he has more in common with his simpatico secretary, Ana Mario Pichio, than with people his own age in Sergio Renan's Argentine masterpiece The Truce *(*La Tregua, 1974*). (Courtesy Buelax Producciones)*

(Hector Alterio, co-star of *The Official Story*) who starts to question the bourgeois values by which he has lived all his life and who finds new meaning for his existence through a lovely affair with his young, simpatico secretary. It's a marvelous relationship with tender love scenes, and the movie as a whole examines bourgeois life with more clarity, depth, humor and honesty than almost all the American movies on the subject from the late 60's to the mid-70's combined.

There were romantic foreign hits as well. One of the biggest was the uproarious French farce *The Tall Blond Man with One Black Shoe* (1972), starring Pierre Richard as a frizzy-haired concert violinist unaware he's being chased by spies. He's also unaware that he's sexually irresistible (he has a charming little boy quality about him), winding up in bed with a passionate woman violinist and a beautiful blonde spy (Mireille Darc). When Darc tells her superior she spent the night making love to Richard, she mutters to herself, "And he was good, too."

A romantic surprise was Claude LeLouche's endearingly offbeat 1973 crime caper *Happy New Year,* in which craggy-faced crook Lino Ventura falls for the free-thinking charmer (Françoise Fabian) who runs

the antique shop next door to the jewelry store he's planning to heist. He's out of place among her academic friends, but she finds his bluff, unschooled intelligence far more sexually arousing than her current lover's pompous intellect, so she and Ventura have a marvelous time in bed.

The late 1970's produced a crop of heterosexual love stories that were alternately wholesome, reassuring, offbeat, electrifying, and downright smutty. United Artists had a string of releases in 1976 that included one of the biggest romantic hits of the decade: *Rocky,* making a star of Sylvester Stallone and proving that there was, in fact, a *huge* audience for old-fashioned moviemaking about an underdog hero and his struggle to become a winner in the boxing ring.

What made *Rocky* click was not that this concept or Stallone's script were original, because they weren't, but that it brought Hollywood back to its populist roots, to a simple, pure fable of ordinary people falling in love and motivating each other to succeed against overwhelming odds; which was how the movie itself got made. Stallone's evolving romance with shy Talia Shire is sincere and tender in its good-heartedly lunky way, and when they finally make love, they give the feeling that here are two lonely, love-starved people reaching out to each other. It was so cornball it worked and had audiences cheering.

Audiences also cheered for dance hall king John Travolta in 1977's big hit *Saturday Night Fever*. Here was a blazingly erotic sex star par excellence as Travolta gyrated around that strobing disco dance floor like a cock-o'-the-walk. Just as Fred Astaire used his fleet feet to woo Ginger Rogers back in the 30'and 40's, Travolta used blatant bumps and grinds to mesmerize Karen Lynn Gorney and Donna Pescow. Travolta became a superstar and the short-lived disco craze was born, all to the tune of pop hits by the Bee Gees.

The late 70's also brought an influx of love stories about emotional crises and the complexities of commitment, in which romance could be sex at first sight, but also a tender evolution of friendship leading to a cozy snuggle in bed. Sex could be painfully complicated, but it could also be warmly familiar.

Two stars who embodied these and other romantic themes were Burt Reynolds and Jill Clayburgh. Reynolds's image was that of the easygoing good old boy who parlays his moustachioed good looks and considerable natural charm and wit into numerous sexual liaisons, both momentary and steady. Clayburgh, on the other hand, embodied the distraught 70's woman on the rebound from a faithless husband in *An Unmarried Woman* (1978), and the hopeful 70's woman trying to find the right man after numerous disappointments and heartaches in *Starting*

Walter Matthau counting piggies with Glenda Jackson in House Calls *(1978).*

Alan Bates seems to be the right kind of sensitive man Jill Clayburgh is searching for in An Unmarried Woman *(1978).*

Clayburgh also wants to make it right with Burt Reynolds in Starting Over (1979)…

…but Reynolds is still attached to ex-wife Candice Bergen. Or is he?

Over (1979), co-starring Reynolds. The appeal of both actors was and is that they are soft-hearted but tough, vulnerable yet resilient, sophisticated but earthy. In short, they are likeable and comfortable to watch.

It's also interesting to compare *An Unmarried Woman* with *Starting Over* because each movie is about a dead marriage and one of the partners seeking therapy to deal with the pain and confusion of divorce. In the former, Clayburgh spills her guts to a psychiatrist while working out a relationship with charming, witty, sensitive painter Alan Bates. In the latter, Reynolds—clean-shaven and speaking in a lower register—tries group therapy to sort out *his* feelings while feeling his way into a relationship with Clayburgh. Clayburgh ends up leaving Bates because she isn't sure she wants to remarry, while Reynolds retreats to ex-wife Candice Bergen because she offers the easy comfort of the familiar past as opposed to the groping uncertainties of a new life with Clayburgh who is much better for him. Though *An Unmarried Woman* is trenchantly realistic in its observations of postmarital distress and its accompanying emotional wariness, offering the seeming honesty of an ambivalent ending, it is too slick and glib and deliberately uncomfortable overall for its own good, sliding over its own surface. In contrast, *Starting Over* is a more comfortable, uplifting film because its style is more relaxed, if less vivid, and you get more of a feeling of living with the characters, of getting to know, like and understand them. The ending is also unsatisfactory and a few scenes don't ring true, but at least the movie is stating that two normal, decent, kindly people can make a go of it at a time when divorce and promiscuity and fear of commitment are the fashions.

There were other simpatico screen romances as well. Caustic feminist Glenda Jackson, for instance, cured doctor Walter Matthau of his errant, swinging ways in *House Calls* (1978), getting him to admit that a long-term relationship with someone his own age is far more rewarding, both to the ego and in bed, than a series of casual affairs with love-starved young women. The sexiest scene in this delightful movie is when Matthau and Jackson decide to see what would happen if they follow the old movie code of making love while one or the other of them has one foot on the floor, conclusively demonstrating the physical impossibility of making love like a human pretzel. They end up on the floor in each other's arms, laughing at the joke they have shared.

Beautiful.

The early to mid-80's brought a variety of other views of man/woman courtships, ranging from the sexually semi-explicit to the cuddly to the distastefully dismal, but generally conveying the idea that adults could still find romantic comfort in traditional match-ups.

One actress during this period who found stardom in the tomboy mold was Debra Winger. Her earthy beauty, easygoing disposition, vulnerability and husky voice brought her an immediate following in movies like *Urban Cowboy* (1981) and *An Officer and a Gentleman* (1982), in both of which she outshone her male co-stars. In the former, she irks lover John Travolta by demonstrating her prowess on the mechanical bull at Gilley's Bar that all the young cowpokes use to prove their virility. In the latter, she is drawn to naval pilot candidate Richard Gere, offering him love and support for his chosen career (she has always wanted to marry a naval pilot). The sexiest scene is an implicitly framed one when she slides on top of him, easing his manhood inside her and her facial expression shows that it feels so good and so right.

Urban Cowboy *(1980): Debra Winger and John Travolta look happily newly married but his insecurity and macho pride soon have them seeking solace with other partners.*

Saul Rubinek nuzzles dream girl Marcia Strassman in Soup for One *(1982).*

One of the neglected gems of this period is *Soup for One* (1982), the debut vehicle for director Jonathan Kaufer, and a fine showcase for actor Saul Rubinek. Rubinek plays a schlemiel who works for an underground cable station and pursues his dream woman, Marcia Strassman, much to her annoyance. He finally wears down her resistance and makes love to her, making her think they may just be right for each other.

What is so very appealing about *Soup for One* is its Jewish waggishness and the puppy dog likeability of Rubinek. He has a nice feel for playing a seeming nerd who knows what he wants and goes for it. The movie got a limited theatrical play and was relegated mainly to cable showings, which is a shame. It's not nearly as good as it could have been—some scenes are alternately hot and cold and there is a lack of chemistry between Rubinek and Strassman—but it certainly deserves more attention if only for Rubinek's central performance.

A foreign delight of the mid-1980's was a romantic comedy from West Germany's Percy Adlon, *Sugarbaby* (1985), which struck a blow for Big Beautiful Women everywhere. Usually, fat women are treated as sexless and emotionally inferior objects of derision in mainstream movies, yet here is a 250-pound mortician's assistant (Marianne Sagebrecht) who is not only a sexual aggressor, but who becomes more radiantly erotic the more she pursues and seduces a slim, blond subway conductor (Eisi Gulp). He gives in to her seduction because he is lonely and bored—he and his attractive wife work different hours and lead separate lives—and because she is sincere and exudes a loving temperament. For all the movie has going for it— mainly Sagebrecht's stunning performance as a homely, fat woman waking up to life from a year's dead existence—it has major technical and scripting problems. Adlon aims for a swooning romantic tone by having the camera pan up, down, left, right and sideways to evoke a mood but all he ends up doing is distracting the viewer to the point of wanting to shout,

Ladies' man Burt Reynolds knows he has made Cynthia Sikes one sexually satisfied woman in The Man Who Loved Women *(1983).*

"Stand still!" Moreover, the ending is elliptically ambiguous and therefore unsatisfying. It's not the payoff you expect or hope for. Despite these flaws, *Sugarbaby's* message is welcome and long overdue: that body size has less to do with what makes a woman—or a man for that matter—beautiful than with the heart and mind concealed by all that weight.

Another chaser, literally, was Burt Reynolds in Blake Edward's remake of Francois Truffaut's *The Man Who Loved Women* (1983). Reynolds plays an inveterate womanizer who compulsively falls for almost every female he meets. They, in turn, fall for him because he is charming, personable and sincere. He is after romance, not just conquest. But, his addiction leads to near-impotence, so he seeks counseling from psychiatrist Julie Andrews, with whom he also falls in love. This sounds comically intriguing, but the truth is that this version is superior to the 1977 Truffaut original in only one respect: Burt Reynolds has screen presence and a sense of humor, both of which Charles

Henry Winkler and Shelley Long share an affectionate post-coital moment in Night-shift *(1982), though she looks a bit happier than he.*

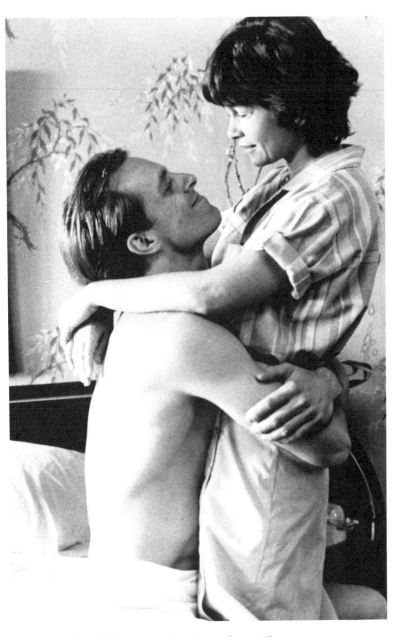

A deceptively appealing pose from Alan Rudolph's dismal Choose Me *(1984). Keith Carradine is a compulsive liar and Genevieve Bujold is a neurotic radio sex therapist. They deserve each other. (Courtesy Island Alive)*

Denner lacks in the original. Truffaut's version is overlong and a trifle dull, but on the whole, it has more verbal wit, visual sophistication and sexual psychology in relating its tale of an all-embracing ladies' man than the Edwards remake, which, in comparison, is intolerably slow and boring.

The most dismal romantic movie of the early 80's was certainly Alan Rudolph's *Choose Me* (1984), which wound up on several Ten Best lists, though God knows why. The movie follows the sex lives of six confused or despicable characters, all of whom keep running into each other. Among these characters is a radio talk show sex therapist (Genevieve Bujold) who has a following despite her coldly monotonal approach (she lacks the elegant compassion of Toni Grant and the whimsical humor of Ruth Westheimer), and who cannot find love herself; the ex-spy/pilot (Keith Carradine) who is a self-righteous, compulsive liar and who smokes so much you swear he's almost eating those cigarettes; and the female bartender (Lesley Ann Warren) who can only fall for men who will use her and leave her. The movie is visually busy but none of it hangs together in a coherent manner. *Choose Me* is one empty "love" story that leaves you wishing all the characters would just go away.

One of the most exhilarating love stories of the early 80's was surely George Roy Hill's lived-in adaptation of John Irving's *The World According to Garp* (1982). Like so many other movies discussed in this book, *Garp* covers a wide sexual range: romance, prostitution, adultery, transexualism and anti-male feminism; all of it forthright and with a bouyant undertone of optimistic humanity in the face of constant tragedy. Robin Williams is sweetly randy as novelist T.S. Garp, a man sunny in disposition but sad in his writing. His marriage to Mary Beth Hurt evolves from a series of playful seductions, blossoming into a rapturous garden of familial joys and woes; wonderful moments of shared passions or of simply gazing at their sleeping children, and scenes of angry recrimination or painful regret. *Garp* is a movie rich with feeling for its characters that tells us life must go on in the face of horrific adversity because of our continual need for closeness. It also reminds us that family life is the most satisfying sexual gift nature can bestow.

Other movies celebrated the joys of sex in middle and old age:

—In *The Grey Fox* (1983), a turn-of-the-century train robber (Richard Farnsworth) struck up a romance with a feminist photographer (Jackie Burroughs). Theirs is a courtly affair between mature adults, evolving with seasoned elegance.

—In *Terms of Endearment* (1985), loneliness and

In The World According to Garp *(1982), aspiring writer Robin Williams falls for Mary Beth Hurt, and she eventually for him, though their life together is earmarked for upheaval, disaster and tragedy.*

Believe it or not, Ryan O'Neal is sharing his passion for movies with moon-eyed doll Shelley Long in Irreconcilable Differences *(1984).*

Newlywed Debra Winger compares notes with…

years of pent-up sexual desire take their toll on fiftiesh Shirley MacLaine, compelling her to give in to the advances of astronaut Jack Nicholson, who turns out to be pretty good in bed.

—And there was Ron Howard's science-fiction saga, *Cocoon* (1985), in which several veteran actors filled the screen with seasoned charm and showed that growing old is no reason to stop making love. After Don Ameche, Hume Cronyn and Wilford Brimley take a swim in a literal fountain of youth, they surprise and delight Gwen Verdon, Jessica Tandy and Maureen Stapleton respectively with their new-found sexual vigor.

The message of all three movies is that sex doesn't have to and shouldn't stop at 40, 50 or any age so long as the people involved care about each other and do what they can to make each other happy in and out of bed.

...mom Shirley MacLaine, who has just had a bout with astronaut Jack Nicholson in Terms of Endearment *(1983). Winger's hubby, Jeff Daniels, is catching up on some reading.*

That is really the point being made by the best of these movies, that fulfilling sexual love between consenting adults of whatever age is always possible no matter how ugly or demented or just plain cockeyed the rest of the world seems to become. For all of the monstrous characters and bloodthirsty violence leaping out of the silver screen to give us nightmares, there is still a plentiful offering of boy-meets-girl and man-meets-women attractions to dream on that glow with warmth, humor, vitality and spunky variety.

No matter how many venal directors there are who are eager to convince us that we are basically worthless, there will always be a dedicated core of sincere filmmakers who know better and who will never let us forget that we have souls as well as sex glands. Most important of all, that erotic stimulation begins in the mind, shoots directly to the heart and *then* works its way downward.

In Ron Howard's science-fantasy adventure, Co-coon (1985), alien woman Tahnee Welch teaches Steve Guttenberg, who loves her, the power of sharing during a ro-mantic swim.

Michael Sarrazin apparently knows exactly what to whisper in Morgan Fairchild's ear in The Seduction *(1982).*

Diane Lane and Thelonius Bernard are kindred spirits riding a gondola to the Bridge of Sighs in A Little Romance *(1979).*

Margot Kidder is literally swept off her feet by Christopher Reeve in Superman II *(1980).*

Love shy Tom Hanks falls for the seductively innocent charm of Daryl Hannah in Splash *(1984) not realizing she is really a mermaid.*

Bo Derek in Greg Benson's Bolero *(1984), a softcore tease that's just plain boring. (Courtesy U.S.A. Home Video)*

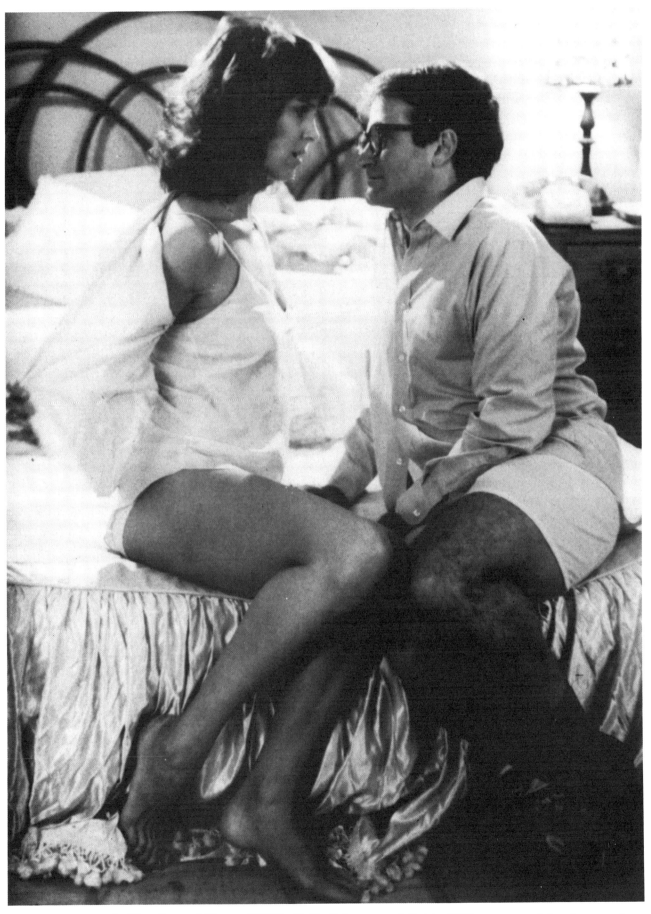

In The Best of Times *(1986), Holly Palance and Robin Williams created heady sexual chemistry as a married couple making the best of life in a godforsaken small town in California.*

In this suggestively sensuous scene from Maria's Lovers *(1984), Nastassja Kinski as Maria ponders the love of John Savage while contemplating commitment to another man.*

HOME VIDEO
RECOMMENDATIONS

In order to write about most of the movies discussed in this book, I just about chained myself to a TV set and VCR for a few months in 1985; it was inevitably an extremely depressing experience. After viewing in one huge three-month lump how sex in cinema has evolved and regressed since 1970, my opinion of world cinema in general and American movies in particular is not a good one. I am convinced that most contemporary screenwriters, directors, producers and especially American studio heads have not only forgotten how to make good, solid, professionally crafted, meaningful narrative films—with large, healthy doses of risk-taking and imagination—but that they have willfully abandoned the legacy of the Golden Age of Movies—roughly the early 1920's through mid-1960's—with the most venal of intents. They have certainly reaped huge financial rewards for pandering to the lowest common denominators among us, but we are immeasurably poorer culturally for this wholesale trashing of one of the world's great mediums of visual art, communication and humanity.

Since most of the movies discussed or depicted in this book are available on cassettes for home viewing, it would be a pointless waste of space to repeat all those titles here. I think the best thing to do is to list those titles which, in my opinion, are worthwhile to rent or buy. In short, the good stuff.

As of press time, a handful of these titles are not yet on home video—two foreign films in my top category aren't available in the United States in any form—but I am listing them anyway because they either soon will be or because I hope that enough interest will be generated by this listing to compel a few of the video companies and some theater owners to make them available.

There are five categories here. Guilty Pleasures are movies that aren't particularly good movies in their own right but which appeal to my bawdy, sleazy

After sharing a powerful climax in Women in Love *(1970), Oliver Reed and Glenda Jackson reflect on their relationship and whether it has any future.*

Kris Kristofferson and Ellen Burstyn kiss with a passion in public in Alice Doesn't Live Here Anymore *(1975).*

side. They are good trashy fun with plenty of good cheap sex. As for the porno titles, as a general rule, almost anything starring Veronica Hart or Colleen Brennan is worth seeing and the titles listed here are the flicks in which they are at their sizzling best, though in some cases the rest of the movie isn't as hot as they are.

The rating system for the mainstream titles is self-explanatory, but for those movies where an individual performance is better than the movie as a whole, I have cited the actor or actors I enjoyed.

For the most part, these are movies that entertained me in varying degrees and which I would happily see again. I know there are critics and buffs who will disagree with my ratings for some of these titles and who will wonder why some were included and others weren't. All I can say in response is that critical disagreements are an occupational hazard and

Handsome, sexy Mel Gib-son has eyes for sexy, sul-try Sigourney Weaver and vice-versa in The Year of Living Dan-gerously *(1982).*

that, after all, this *is* a Critic's Choice list. If most or even a handful of these titles give you pleasure, uplift and insight, the list will have served its modest purpose as a personalized reference guide to the best of sex in cinema since 1970.

While most of these titles are readily available at most video stores, some homosexual-themed titles may not be. The best source for ordering homosexual-themed movies or movies with gay appeal is Award Films at 525 N. Laurel Ave., Los Angeles, CA 90048, 213-462-5997. The person to write to is Tim Wohlgemuth, who will happily track down any gay appeal title(s) you are looking for, no matter how obscure. Award Films specialty items are designated by AF. Also, if any of these titles have been withdrawn by the time this book is in print, one shop that can special order for you is Video West in North Hollywood.

Finally, the name of the video distributor follows the year of release to help in renting or buying these titles.

GUILTY PLEASURES
THE BIG BIRD CAGE (1970, Warner)
DEATH RACE 2000 (1975, Warner)
IT'S NOT THE SIZE THAT COUNTS (1974, Embassy)
PORKY'S (1981, CBS/Fox)
UP! (1975)

PORNO MOVIES
AMANDA BY NIGHT (1982, Caballero) w/Veronica Hart, R. Bolla and Jamie Gillis
AMERICAN DESIRE (1982, Caballero) w/Veronica Hart and R. Bolla
BODY GIRLS (1984, VCA) w/Hyapatia Lee
CENTERFOLD FEVER (1982, Video-X-Pix) w/Marc "10 ½" Stevens, Lisa Be and Ron Jeremy
DELICIOUS (1981, Video-X-Pix) w/Veronica Hart
EVERY WOMAN HAS A FANTASY (1984, VCA) w/John Leslie and Rachel Ashley
GAMES WOMEN PLAY (1981, TVX) w/Veronica Hart
INDECENT EXPOSURE (1982, Caballero) w/Veronica Hart and Eric Edwards
MATINEE IDOL (1985, VCA) w/Colleen Brennan
THE OPENING OF MISTY BEETHOVEN (1976, VCA) w/ Jamie Gillis and Constance Money
THE PRIVATE AFTERNOONS OF PAMELA MANN (1974, VCA) w/Barbara Bourbon and Marc Stevens
ROOMMATES (1982, Video-X-Pix) w/Veronica Hart, Jerry Butler and Jack Wrangler
SEX DEVICES (1974)
STIFF COMPETITION (1985, Caballero) w/Kevin James and Gina Carrera

Michael Douglas grabs hold of Kathleen Turner in this publicity pose for Romancing the Stone *(1984). It's a wonder they kept a straight face, and no wonder this shot was cropped for newspapers.*

James Garner finally shows his love for Sally Field in Murphy's Ro- *mance (1985) with a kiss that's all the more power- ful for being the only one after several reels of easy- going buildup.*

Jacqueline Bisset has her doubts about marrying young lover Hart Bochner in Rich and Famous *(1981).*

GOOD GIRL, BAD GIRL (1984, Essex) w/Colleen Brennan

TOWER OF POWER (1985, VCA) w/Colleen Brennan

TRINITY BROWN (1985, Cal Vista) w/Colleen Brennan, Jerry Butler and Jamie Gillis

WANDA WHIPS WALL STREET (1982, Video-X-Pix) w/ Veronica Hart

* = Good or Recommended

ALL THE RIGHT MOVES (1983, CBS/Fox)

AVANTI (1972)

THE BEST OF TIMES (1986, Embassy)

COCOON (1985, Fox) for Don Ameche, Hume Cronyn, Jessica Tandy and Gwen Verdon

THE COLOR PURPLE (1985) especially for Whoopi

THE DAY OF THE JACKAL (1973, Warner)

DIVINE MADNESS (1980, Warner)

AN EARLY FROST (1985)

THE GREY FOX (1983, Media Home Entertainment)

HALLOWEEN (1978, Media Home Entertainment)

HAPPY NEW YEAR (1973)

HONEYSUCKLE ROSE (1980, Warner)

I LOVE YOU ALICE B. TOKLAS (1968, Warner)

IRRECONCILABLE DIFFERENCES (1984, Vestron)

THE KENTUCKY FRIED MOVIE (1977)

MICKI AND MAUDE (1984, RCA/Columbia)

MURPHY'S ROMANCE (1985)

NO SMALL AFFAIR (1984, RCA/Columbia) for Jonathan Cryer

OUTRAGEOUS (1977, RCA/Columbia) AF

A QUESTION OF LOVE (1978, IVE) AF

RISKY BUSINESS (1983, Warner)

THE ROCKY HORROR PICTURE SHOW (1975) for Tim Curry

ROMANCING THE STONE (1984, CBS/Fox)

SAME TIME NEXT YEAR (1978, MCA)

SATURDAY NIGHT FEVER (1977, Paramount)

LE SEX SHOP (1975, RCA/Columbia)

SLEEPER (1973, CBS/Fox)

SOUP FOR ONE (1982, Warner) for Saul Rubinek

STARTING OVER (1979, Paramount)

SUGARBABY (1985) for Marianne Sagebrecht

SUMMER OF '42 (1971, Warner)

TEN (1979, Warner)

A TOUCH OF CLASS (1973, CBS/Fox)

URBAN COWBOY (1980, Paramount)

VICE SQUAD (1981, Embassy)

VICTOR/VICTORIA (1982, MGM) especially for Robert Preston

YOUNG FRANKENSTEIN (1974, CBS/Fox)

** = Very good or Must-see

ALICE DOESN'T LIVE HERE ANYMORE (1975, Warner)
AMARCORD (1974, Warner)
BACK TO THE FUTURE (1985, MCA)
LA CAGE AUX FOLLES (1978, CBS/Fox) AF
COUSIN, COUSINE (1975, CBS/Fox)
EATING RAOUL (1982, CBS/Fox)
GET OUT YOUR HANDKERCHIEFS (1978, Warner)
THE GODFATHER (1972, Paramount)
HAROLD AND MAUDE (1971, Paramount)
HOUSE CALLS (1978, MCA)
KISS OF THE SPIDER WOMAN (1985, Charter Entertainment) especially for William Hurt
KLUTE (1971, Warner)
A LITTLE ROMANCE (1979, Warner)
MURMUR OF THE HEART (1971)
THE MUSIC LOVERS (1971)
NETWORK (1976, MGM)
NIGHT SHIFT (1982, Warner)
THE PURPLE ROSE OF CAIRO (1985, Vestron)
SOMETHING ABOUT AMELIA (1984)
SOUNDER (1972, Paramount)
SPLASH (1984, Touchstone/Disney)
SUPERMAN (1978, Warner)
THE SURE THING (1985, Embassy)
TAKING OFF (1971)
THE TALL BLOND MAN WITH ONE BLACK SHOE (1972, RCA/Columbia)
THAT CERTAIN SUMMER (1972)
TRADING PLACES (1983, Paramount)
WOMEN IN LOVE (1970, CBS/Fox)

*** = Excellent, Classic, Knockout

ANNIE HALL (1977, CBS/Fox)
BODY HEAT (1981, Warner)
CARNAL KNOWLEDGE (1971, Embassy)
CHINATOWN (1973, Paramount)
EL DIPUTADO (THE DEPUTY, 1979 Award Films)
FOR LADIES ONLY (1981, USA Home Video)
GREAT! (1975)
HUSTLING (1975, Worldvision)
LIANNA (1983, Vestron) AF
THE NAKED CIVIL SERVANT (1975, Thorne/EMI) AF
PIXOTE (1981, RCA/Columbia) AF
PLAY IT AGAIN, SAM (1972, Paramount)
TERESA THE THIEF (1975)
THE TRUCE (LE TREGUA, 1974)
WOODSTOCK (1970, Warner)
THE WORLD ACCORDING TO GARP (1982, Warner)

(Far right)

Alien visitor Jeff Bridges in Starman *(1984) is enamored of widowed earthling Karen Allen. She returns his affection because he is a dead ringer for her dead husband.*

218